taste
healthy, hearty asian recipes

taste

healthy, hearty asian recipes

sylvia tan

Marshall Cavendish
Cuisine

Editor: Sylvy Soh
Designer: Rachel Chen
Photographer: Joshua Tan, Elements by the Box

Text © 2009 Sylvia Tan
Photographs © 2009 Marshall Cavendish International (Asia)
Private Limited

Published by Marshall Cavendish Cuisine
An imprint of Marshall Cavendish International
1 New Industrial Road, Singapore 536196

Other Marshall Cavendish Offices:
Marshall Cavendish Ltd.5th Floor, 32–38 Saffron Hill, London
EC1N 8FH • Marshall Cavendish Corporation. 99 White Plains
Road, Tarrytown NY 10591-9001, USA • Marshall Cavendish
International (Thailand) Co Ltd. 253 Asoke, 12th Flr, Sukhumvit
21 Road, Klongtoey Nua, Wattana, Bangkok 10110, Thailand •
Marshall Cavendish (Malaysia) Sdn Bhd, Times Subang, Lot 46,
Subang Hi-Tech Industrial Park, Batu Tiga, 40000 Shah Alam,
Selangor Darul Ehsan, Malaysia

Marshall Cavendish is a trademark of Times Publishing Limited

National Library Board Singapore Cataloguing in Publication
Data

Tan, Sylvia.
Taste: healthy, hearty Asian recipes / Sylvia Tan. Singapore :
Marshall Cavendish Cuisine, 2009.
p. cm.
Includes index.
ISBN-13 : 978-981-261-853-5
ISBN-10 : 981-261-853-8

1. Low-fat diet – Recipes. 2. Salt-free diet – Recipes.
3. Cookery, Asian. I. Title.

TX714
641.563 -- dc22   OCN320281508

Printed in Singapore by KWF Printing Pte Ltd

for my husband,

kay tong,

who appreciates fine
food in its truest sense.

contents

introduction

This is a collection of my favourite recipes that I cook regularly for family and friends. They are delicious and interesting enough even for people for whom taste, and not health, is paramount.

And when I serve them, no one even thinks of them as health food, for not only do I use whole grains and vegetables, I also cook up umami-rich ingredients such as artichokes, crabmeat, mushrooms, salmon, avocado, seaweed… even pork, lamb and beef.

Contrary to popular misconceptions, all these foods are healthy, depending on the cut you use, if it's meat, and the method of cooking.

None of the recipes is difficult; all of them appeal to our Asian tastes and many have become firm family favourites, despite their healthy label!

People are concerned about their health and well-being. From my informal observations, many are making changes, albeit small, to their diet – whether it is eating brown rice, using healthier oils for cooking or removing obvious fat from meats.

The changes may be small but they are a start.

In my family, the first step we took was to change from white rice to brown rice… slowly, by first adding a little, then more, and finally, by replacing white rice entirely.

From this, we have now expanded the range of healthy choices in our daily meals. Today, our carbohydrate intake is drastically reduced, we use only monounsaturated oils for cooking, we eat more fish, and at every meal, there are at least two vegetable dishes on the table.

While the changes have been slow, they have been certain and today, we eat meals that definitely more healthy than a few years ago.

A few principles emerge when cooking for health.

We would poach or steam rather than fry, we would choose the fillets of meat, which are leaner, more tender but still tasty. We would use spices lavishly for they add interest for the palate. We skim every broth we use, for this would mean less fat and no sacrifice of taste.

These are not changes that are difficult to make. These are changes we can live with… for life.

soups

soup

soups are the mainstay of eating in my home. just as our mothers lovingly made double-boiled soups when anyone was feeling under the weather, i too resort to soup nutrition. there are cooling soups for an over-heated body, and warming soups for strength. today, i also make soups, when i want a light meal, need a first course or when i want to poach some vegetables, a piece of meat or fish. easily defatted, it is the cornerstone of a low-fat diet.

fish and pineapple soup

Nothing does it like hot soup during cool rainy days. Whether it is global warming or not, we are having such cool days that I have started to serve piping hot soups to ward off the chill in the air!

But despite the cool nights, I feel soups have to be light, snappy and tangy if you're living in the tropics. This one–a fish and pineapple soup with Southeast Asian flavours fits the bill.

Rich in protein, it uses snapper, which is ideal food. Snapper is low-fat and one of the few fishes that are relatively low in mercury. It also has a mild flavour. I tire of the strongly flavoured rich fishes such as salmon and cod, though they are popular. Despite being high in cholesterol (some 37 mg per serve of 100 g [3½ oz]), snapper's count is still lower than salmon's 68 mg per 100 g (3½ oz).

The sourness comes from tamarind, lifted by handfuls of fresh mint and basil leaves. Despite the spice, it is not so overpowering that it cannot be eaten on its own.

To choose fish, I like to go to the wet market, for then I can look at, touch and smell the fish. I also adore the whole experience of finding fish that glisten with freshness. They almost demand to be eaten, unlike plastic-wrapped fish from the supermarket, which look so characterless. When purchasing a whole snapper, look for a shiny skin and a good red or pink colour. The belly cavity should also glisten and smell of the ocean, which is not the same as smelling fishy.

Similarly, the pineapple should be choice. I like to buy it from the cut fruit stall for they always offer sweet fruit. A sweet fruit is essential to balance the sourness of the tamarind, even if its sourness is not as sharp as vinegar. Tomatoes add colour (and they should also be ripe!) as do cut red chillies and the fresh mint, basil and coriander. Be brave and add whole handfuls to the bowl.

Snapper fish 400 g (14⅓ oz), deboned

Cut pineapple 3 slices

Tamarind paste or purée 1 Tbsp

Water or chicken or fish stock 5 cups

Tomatoes 4–6, cut into quarters

Fish sauce 1 Tbsp

Salt a pinch

Sugar 1 tsp

Basil, coriander and mint leaves 1 bunch each

Red chillies (optional) 2–3, sliced

1. Cut fish and pineapple into thick slices. Season fish with a little of the fish sauce and leave aside.

2. Dissolve tamarind paste in a cup of water. Strain to remove seeds and fibres or else use tamarind purée, available in jars or packets.

3. Add water or stock to make up 5 cups of liquid and bring to the boil. Add pineapple slices and tomato quarters and when it comes to the boil again, add fish slices.

4. Season with remaining fish sauce, salt and sugar and taste to adjust seasoning if needed. Just before serving, divide fish, pineapple and tomatoes among four bowls and garnish with generous amounts of fresh basil, coriander and mint leaves. Add chilli slices if desired and serve at once.

5. To make a more substantial meal, you can add boiled thick rice noodles to the bowl as well. Make sure you adjust the seasoning again. This makes a warming soup in more ways than one on cool nights.

serves 4-5

kiam chye duck soup

Everyone loves *kiam chye* soup. Add a bunch of the salted mustard leaves to a pot and it gives a pungent salty sweetness to the soup. My nephews drink it by the bowlfuls, shovelling lots of rice after. Yet think about the salt content in those bowls!

Pickled in salt, then left to ferment, these mustard leaves were preserved in such a manner in China to keep them for periods of scarcity. A repertoire of recipes arose just for salted vegetables.

Today, it is a different story. People eat salted vegetable soup because they love it. Of the soups, this one is a classic—a salted vegetable soup cooked with duck, better known as *itek teem* or *kiam chye ap*. While this soup can be cooked with pork bones or a whole fish head, it is the duck soup that holds top position. The briny mustard leaves (and the sour plums, a classic match) add piquancy to a rich broth. The Peranakans, in their inimitable way, add a whole pig's trotter as well to the pot and serve it with a splash of cognac and a garnish of green chilli, when it makes its appearance every Chinese New Year! No one worried then about high sodium intake nor fat levels. All told, something needed to be done to make this classic less harmful.

Well, I have worked out a healthier recipe. While it needs some preparation overnight, it means that I need not forgo this customary delight. I skin the whole duck then parboil it. The skin after all is where most of the fat resides. This also makes the bird less gamey. Parboiling the duck makes it easy to de-fat the soup. I then leave the stock to chill in the fridge overnight. A layer of fat solidifies on the surface, making it easy to remove the next day. I then cook with this defatted stock. Not only that, I use fresh, not salted, mustard leaves. Of course, I salt the broth as usual, but it will not have the same salt levels as the original. More importantly, it is the sour plums that give the soup its characteristic piquancy.

So I use it to flavour the soup but fresh tomatoes can also give that zing. Everything else remains— and so I add as well, dried tamarind slices, a whole head of garlic, a knob of ginger and yes, that final dash of cognac and snapped green chillies. And believe me, few will know the difference.

Whole duck 1, about 2 kg (4 lb 6 oz)

Cognac about 1–2 Tbsp

Fresh mustard leaves 1–2 heads, about 500 g (1 lb 1½ oz) (add more if you like), cut into large pieces

Unpeeled ginger 1 thumb-sized knob

Unpeeled garlic 1 head

Dried tamarind 4 slices

Sour plums 4

Salt 1 tsp

Sugar 1 tsp

Light soy sauce 1 tsp or to taste

Tomatoes 5, cut into quarters

Green chillies 2–3

1. Ask the poultry seller to remove the skin from the duck. Prepare bird by rubbing cognac well into its flesh.

2. Place duck in a pot and cover with water. Bring to the boil, then remove from heat. Cool and place the pot in the fridge overnight.

3. The next day, a solid layer of fat would have formed on top. Remove it carefully. Cut the parboiled duck into 6–8 pieces and return to the defatted stock. Bring to the boil with the mustard leaves.

4. Wash well the unpeeled ginger, garlic head and tamarind slices. Smash ginger to release its juices, then add to the pot, along with garlic and tamarind slices.

5. Bring everything to the boil and after 10 minutes, reduce the heat to a simmer. Season with salt, sugar and light soy sauce. Leave to cook for about 1½ hours or until tender.

6. Finally, add tomatoes. Add a splash of cognac and those snapped green chillies, before serving. And there you have it, a traditional soup updated to serve today's health concerns.

serves 8

chinese minestrone

The Chinese have a commendable habit for the New Year. They go vegetarian at least for the first day. It is like a cleansing of the mind and body in preparation for the year ahead. This vegetable soup goes part of the way. Not entirely vegetarian as it relies on chicken stock and uses ham to flavour, it is still ideal food after the excesses of the season, being clean, light and tasty. And on the morning after, it is also important to know that it is easy to prepare, taking less than an hour, if you have the stock on hand.

What vegetables to include? Since this is a soup that celebrates the seasons, you really should pick vegetables that are in season such as Chinese cabbage (*bok choy*), which is a winter vegetable, at least in China.

Here I am opting for a 'green' soup. Less well-known than the red tomato-based minestrone, the flavours of the vegetables seem to sing through here, unclouded by the rich taste of tomato. Minestrone traditionally relies on beans and a leafy vegetable. For this Chinese version, I use fresh green soy beans or *edamame*, Thai asparagus and yes, a leafy *bok choy*. I also include some Chinese cured ham and rice wine instead of Italian bacon and white wine to keep to the oriental theme.

All three vegetables are rich in vitamins (especially A and C) fibre and minerals. Soy beans in particular are a good source of protein. When cooking a vegetable soup, timing is of the essence to preserve the bright green colours of the vegetables. So undercooking is a good way to go; remember that the residual heat will continue to cook any greens added to the pot, finishing it off nicely.

For any soup, the stock is important.

While you could rely on store-bought organic stock to save time, a stock made with a whole chicken is a true luxury. Just boil a chicken with some onions, leeks, carrots and celery, simmering for an hour. Use the stock but keep the flesh for another use later. Do this in advance.

While Italian soups may include a tortellini or two floating in the broth, here I add a couple of chive dumplings (frozen is convenient). What could be more comforting than dumplings in soup especially on a New Year's morning?

Olive oil 1 tsp

Small onion 1, chopped finely

Garlic 1 clove, chopped finely

Carrot 1, diced

Celery 1 stalk, diced

Chinese (Yunnan) ham 4 thin slices, diced

Rice wine ½ cup

Chicken or vegetable stock (see article) 1.5 litres (48 fl oz / 6 cups)

Store-bought frozen chive dumplings (optional) 10-12

Fresh soy beans (*edamame*) 200 g (7 oz), removed from pods

Thai asparagus spears 15, cut into short lengths

Chinese cabbage (*bok choy*) 1 bunch, shredded

1. Heat olive oil in a pot and fry onion and garlic until softened. Add carrot, celery and ham and cook for 5 minutes.

2. Add rice wine and simmer to evaporate the alcohol. Pour in stock and boil for about 5 minutes more.

3. Add dumplings. When they float to the surface, remove with a slotted spoon and set aside.

4. Add soy beans and cook for a further 5 minutes, followed by asparagus and *bok choy* for three minutes, allowing them to just wilt.

5. Remove from heat and serve at once, topped with a couple of dumplings per serving. A more pristine meal you could not find!

serves 4-6

soy bean shreds soup

Shredded silk. That was what I thought when I first encountered this clear soup in which floated shreds of snow-white soy bean skin.

I was in Nanjing, China on a flying visit so I only had time for quick sorties into restaurants to try out their specialties that included in one, a boiled fertilised egg, chicken embryo and all!

But this bowl of soy bean skin was different. It looked and tasted beautiful. The bean skin had been cut into fine strips and had then been poached gently in a broth redolent with the scent of the most fragrant Chinese ham. I had never eaten a soup like this one. Yes, it was a tofu soup in a sense, but the tofu here was not a curd, but rather the bean skin that forms on top of the curd. A triumph of textures, it was soft and silky, with every mouthful impregnated with the flavour of the most superior stock, made with chicken and ham. And best of all, it was healthy as it was clear of any oil. Instead, the main ingredient was the bean skin.

Soy bean sheets are generally sold dried though you can also obtain it fresh, if you're lucky. Some soy bean (tofu and *tau kwa*) stalls in the wet markets sell the fresh skin, stored in their refrigerator, so you will have to ask for it. Otherwise you can also buy the dried sheets, but do be aware that there are two kinds. One is the thicker salted version that is often used as a wrap, while the other is the softer and finer version used for that favourite cooling sweet bean skin and barley soup. This second skin is what is needed for this soup. It gives us yet another delicious way of eating soy bean. Of course the other important component is the stock and for this, I would make my own, adding some cubes of Chinese ham to flavour the pot.

I also added some fresh green soy beans (also sold frozen in packets in supermarkets) and fresh shiitake mushroom slivers to the broth. It gives a welcome contrast to the otherwise snowy-white landscape of this beautiful soup.

Canned or homemade unsalted chicken stock (see method) 6 cups

Dried soft soy bean skin 1 sheet

Chinese (Yunnan) ham 1 medium slice, diced

Fresh soy beans (*edamame*) 1 cup, boiled, then removed from pods

Fresh shiitake mushrooms 5, cut into slivers, or use dried shiitake mushrooms reconstituted in water for 30 minutes

Rice wine 1 Tbsp

Salt 1 tsp

Ground white pepper to taste

Sugar 1 pinch

1. To make chicken stock from scratch, place 2–3 chicken carcasses, 2 carrots, 1 celery stalk and 1 onion in a pot. Cover with water and bring to the boil, then simmer for an hour. Strain and reserve stock for use later.

2. Soak soy bean skin in water until it softens. Roll it up, then steam in covered wok half-filled with water for 15 minutes. Remove from wok and set aside.

3. In a pot, bring stock to the boil. Add half of diced ham, then add rice wine, shiitake mushroom slivers and remaining seasonings.

4. Add soy bean skin roll and poach gently for 30 minutes until it softens. Remove from pot, cool and cut into strips. Taste stock to adjust seasoning if needed.

5. Divide bean strips into 4–6 bowls. Top with green soy beans, then pour over the broth. Serve at once.

serves 4-6

fish with grated radish soup

Look, there is no fat in this soup! But taste it, it is delectable. The flavour would have come not from fat but from the fish, in this case, a threadfin, or *ikan kurau* fillet. This sweet-tasting fish would have been cooked in a dashi stock, which is nothing more than seaweed and dried bonito flakes. And in this case, the stock would have heightened by a dollop of raw grated radish, all coming together to create a memorable fish soup.

The lack of fat in this soup is no accident. It is a Japanese soup and there is no fat or oil in most Japanese traditional foods. In fact, I would look to Japanese food after a period of feasting to lighten my eating.Japanese cookbook author Kimiko Barber goes a step further when she recommends eating Japanese food as a way of keeping healthier and slimmer. She says the Japanese are able to do this, because they use chopsticks, and that physically slows down the eating (or prevents gobbling, in my book)!

They also eat with the eyes. Their food comes beautifully and artistically presented, making you pause before you take yet another mouthful. And of course their diet is high in fibre-rich foods such as vegetables, rice, soba noodles and beans, which keep you full longer and lowers the cholesterol. If all this does not convince you, a taste of this soup made with fat-free dashi definitely will.

Dashi is the basic stock in Japanese cuisine. Rather like the familiar *ikan bilis* and soy bean stock, dashi is also made from dried fish—bonito flakes, in this instance, with the giant kelp, *kombu*, adding an extra layer of flavour. Dashi is also simple to make—no long simmering to extract the flavour. Indeed quick cooking is the key, otherwise bitterness would exude from the seaweed. The proportion of seaweed to fish is however important to the final taste. Generally, the recommendation is 1:6; I used 10 g (⅓ oz) *kombu* to 60 g (2 oz) dried bonito flakes.

Once done, all that is needed is to cook the fish and mushrooms quickly in the stock and top it with a generous spoonful of raw grated radish. Yes, raw. Aside from the vitamins (B6, C, fibre and many minerals) the raw vegetable brings to the broth, this final flourish adds taste, flavour and body to the soup without any effort at all.

DASHI STOCK

Dried kelp (*kombu*) 10 g (⅓ oz)

Water 1.5 litres (48 fl oz / 6 cups)

Dried bonito flakes 60 g (2 oz)

Light soy sauce 1 tsp

Salt to taste

Sweet Japanese rice wine (*mirin*) 4 Tbsp

Sugar to taste

INGREDIENTS

Threadfin (*ikan kurau*) steaks 2, each cut in half and rubbed with salt

Willow mushrooms 1 punnet, ends trimmed

Small white radish 1

Spring onion (scallion) 1, chopped

DIPPING SAUCE (COMBINE INGREDIENTS)

Spring onion (scallion) 1, thinly sliced on the diagonal

Red chillies 2, sliced

Lemon juice to taste

Light soy sauce to taste

1. Prepare dashi stock. Wipe kelp with a damp cloth to remove surface dirt. Place in a pot and add water. Heat and remove kelp just before water boils. Bring water to the boil, then add bonito flakes. Skim off any scum that rises to the surface, and turn off the heat. Leave aside to infuse.

2. Strain stock through a sieve. Season to taste with soy sauce, salt, sugar and mirin. Both kelp and bonito flakes can be recycled to make a second stock, with a fresh small piece of kelp.

3. Return dashi stock to the boil, then reduce heat and bring to a simmer. Add threadfin pieces, followed by mushrooms. Simmer for five minutes or until just cooked. Taste and adjust seasoning if desired.

4. Remove fish and mushrooms and divide among four bowls. Spoon stock over. Add a dollop of fresh grated radish. Garnish with chopped spring onion.

5. Serve immediately, with dipping sauce on the side.

serves 4

vegetables and salads

you should aim for lots of variety and colour on your plate, easily met by eating five helpings of fruit and vegetables a day! the vegetables should be as colourful as possible to up your intake of protective foods (antioxidants). recent research also shows that a healthy diet should include at least 30 different kinds of foods a day to get the necessary vitamins and minerals. but it is not challenging as you think, for a stir-fry like the spring stir-fry (see page 34) would already have some seven varieties of foods in it.

vegetables

black and white fungus salad

What could be more dramatic than black and white on a plate? You can get this effect by simply choosing ingredients with those colours for a dish. No mere affectation, the restaurants know how important colour is to presentation and appetites, which is why red fruit, yellow lemon or green parsley can always find a place on their plates.

As for that dramatic black and white combination, I came across it in a Chinese restaurant. They used reconstituted dried black and white fungus, which they flavoured with a sesame dressing and presented as an appetiser. It was not only good to look at, but also good to eat and healthy to boot! I took the idea further, turning the cold appetiser into a full-sized salad, scattered with red wolfberries for added contrast. It was pretty as a picture, plus there are many health benefits.

My aunts say that white fungus is the poor man's alternative to expensive bird's nest as it has the same ameliorating and moisturising properties, but I could find no evidence of this. Instead I discovered that both fungi, black and white, have anti-coagulant properties, making them good for those suffering from atherosclerosis. The black fungus, also known as jelly fungus, cloud's ears and wood ears as it grows from tree trunks, is also rich in protein and iron.

Apparently it has 7 times more iron as pig's liver, which is why it is also known as a good blood tonic increasing the fluidity and circulation of blood, according to traditional Chinese medicine practitioners.

And there is more: Snow fungus or *bai mu er*, literally white wood ear, also has much iron, Vitamin C, calcium and phosphorous. It is also believed to be nourishing for the lungs and can lower 'bad' cholesterol levels or LDL, lower density lipoprotein.

Here it is served uncooked: merely softened in hot water, then dressed before chilling. It then tops a salad of butter lettuce or similarly soft lettuce leaves, adding interest to every mouthful.

It belongs to that rare group of Asian salads, and makes a nice complement to roasted meats and Asian meals.

Dried black fungus 4 pieces

Dried white fungus 1 head

Roasted sesame oil 1 tsp

Light soy sauce ½ tsp

Salt a pinch

Butter lettuce 2 heads

Dried wolfberries 1 Tbsp, reconstituted
in water to soften

DRESSING

Olive oil ½ cup

Roasted sesame oil 1 tsp

Light soy sauce 1 tsp

Limes 2–4, squeezed for juice (choose amount
of limes depending on your taste preference)

White sugar 1 tsp

Salt ½ tsp

Pepper to taste

1. Soak black and white fungus in hot water till they swell. Trim off hard bits and cut into smaller pieces. Drain well.

2. Season with sesame oil, soy sauce and salt. Leave covered in the fridge for flavours to develop.

3. Separate and wash lettuce leaves. Dry them thoroughly.

4. Make up dressing in a separate container, whisking to emulsify.

5. When well combined, add to the lettuce leaves and toss in a separate bowl, transferring later to a serving bowl, to prevent an overdressed soggy salad.

6. Top with seasoned fungi and red wolfberries and there you have it: Dramatic black and white on a plate, contrasted by a touch of red. Who says healthy is colourless?

serves 6

green eating

A whole new world of eating has opened up for me—think about eating vegetables and whole grains, sans salt, sugar and oil! It is a shock to the system, especially when all my life, I have cooked with the aim of maximum taste rather than maximum health. It has been a real challenge, producing meals that follow such principles and yet are tasty at the end of it all. The reason for such discipline? Someone close to me has fallen ill, and has turned to nutritional therapy for help.

Surprisingly, I have discovered that it is not too difficult to cook such food even for the whole family, provided there is salt on the table for others. There are lots of delicious dishes that can be turned out without breaking the rules. I have made *nori* cabbage rolls, *popia*, minestrone soup, *chap chye*, even *sayur lodeh* (using soy milk) and yes, lots of salads and vegetable soups as well.

Belatedly, I found out that lots of people eat in this way basing their meals on whole grains, beans, fruit and vegetables. And if they are strictly macrobiotic, they will not eat meat, fish, dairy foods and use little seasoning except for miso, sea salt and naturally fermented soy sauce in their food. The impact of nutritional therapy on my family has been amusing. My meat-loving son is in a severe state of deprivation and has been reduced to begging for a meat dish whenever we eat out. I also discovered how many vegetable haters there are in my immediate circle, who suddenly have lots of excuses why they cannot eat with us!

The new way of eating has however not prevented us from enjoying our favourite activity of eating out, nor abated our intense interest in food, though these days the discussion would be on how to make a macrobiotic *mee rebus* or laksa! Surprisingly, too many restaurants here do not have a vegetarian option. Consequently it has been hilarious trying to get the kitchens to prepare something vegetarian and…with little salt! Yet Italian salads are delicious, such as this one where I substitute soy bean curd for the mozzarella. I also dripped a rich pesto over the lot, making it a full-tasting salad that should satisfy even meat eaters.

pesto, tofu and tomato salad

Round bean curd 1 roll, about 250 g (9 oz)

Tomatoes 4

PESTO

Basil leaves a bunch

Peeled almonds ½ cup

Garlic 1 clove

Olive oil ½ cup

Sea salt to taste

1. Unwrap soy bean curd and leave in the refrigerator for a few hours to drain. Meanwhile, slice tomatoes thickly. Remove bean curd from the fridge and slice evenly. Lay slices on a plate, interspersed with tomato slices.

2. Process basil leaves, together with almonds, garlic and olive oil in the food processor until fine. Leave aside for a while to allow flavours to infuse.

3. Just before serving, drizzle basil oil over the tomato and soy bean slices. Grind some black pepper over and add a pinch of sea salt.

sliced radish and orange salad

White radish 1, left unpeeled and sliced thinly

Oranges 2, peeled and sliced thinly

Fresh mint leaves a handful

Extra virgin olive oil for drizzling

Crushed black pepper to taste

Sea salt to taste

1. Lay radish slices on a plate. Intersperse the radish slices with orange slices and top everything with fresh mint leaves, torn into little bits.

2. Drizzle olive oil over the lot. Add black pepper and a pinch of sea salt to taste. If liked, you can heighten the orange flavour by adding a few drops of orange oil (get this from the gourmet shops). This gives you another quick salad that is thoroughly refreshing at any time.

serves 2

mushroom and potato parcels

Good things come in little parcels. This is especially true when the parcels contain delicious morsels of chicken, as in paper-wrapped chicken, or in this case, of mushrooms and potatoes.

This, and other vegetarian combinations are my foods of choice after a surfeit, which inevitably occurs during a festive season.

Cooking food in small parcels also means that I can easily control portion sizes, another route of mine after festive indulgence. As for going vegetarian, when the parcel contains mushrooms, the taste quotient rises, thanks to the ample umami component found in the fungi.

For those who do not know, umami is the fifth taste, aside from salty, sweet, sour and bitter, discovered in 1908 by Kikunae Ikeda. a Japanese scientist. Mushrooms, of course, but also cheese, bacon and anchovies, for example, contain large quantities of umami, which accounts for their large flavours.

So this vegetarian parcel will be full of tasty flavours, thanks to the inclusion of large, meaty mushrooms, now found everywhere in the market. I would bake them teamed with russet potatoes, which absorb flavours well. The mushrooms also do not exude much water, making it ideal for baking in paper.

Choose mushrooms without blemishes. To prepare, slice off the hard bit at the bottom of the stem and rinse quickly under a tap. Dry and then slice.

You can bake the mushrooms with olive oil, salt and pepper. Or even with soy or oyster sauce and pepper. It takes just 15 minutes and no mess as it is all cooked in the oven. If you have truffle-flavoured oil, sprinkle some over and the whole bundle becomes not an exercise of restraint, but rather of luxurious consumption!

Abalone mushrooms 2–3, or use king oyster mushrooms (*eryngii*)

Medium-sized russet potatoes 2–3

Garlic 1 clove, peeled and chopped

Salt 1 tsp

Crushed black pepper 1 tsp

Extra virgin olive oil 1 tsp

Truffle-flavoured oil (optional) 1 tsp

Greaseproof oven paper four
    15-cm x 15-cm sheets

Fresh parsley 1 bunch, chopped

1. Preheat oven to 180°C (350°F).

2. Slice off the hard bottom of the mushrooms and rinse them quickly under a running tap. Dry with kitchen towels. Break off cap and slice stem into 1-cm (½-in) pieces on a diagonal. Place sliced mushrooms in a large basin.

3. Peel potatoes and soak them in water to prevent them from turning brown. Slice into 1-cm (½-in) thick slices. Place in the same bowl as mushrooms. Add garlic.

4. Season mushrooms and potato slices with salt and pepper, and drizzle extra-virgin olive oil and truffle-flavoured oil, if desired. Toss to coat the slices well.

5. Divide potatoes and mushrooms into four portions. Place each portion in the centre of each square of grease-proof paper. Gather up the ends of the paper and secure with a stapler.

6. Place bundles on a pan and bake for 15 minutes. Remove and allow each diner to open his parcel. Offer some fresh parsley as garnish and a green salad on the side.

serves 4

roasted capsicums and peitan salad

In case you have not heard, eggs have come in from the cold. My grandfather, who used to take an egg a day has been proven right after all. Researchers from Yale have found that eating eggs every day does not increase bad cholesterol in the blood. They found that while cholesterol in food can raise cholesterol in blood, the response varies from person to person. In about 70 per cent of humans, the body compensates for the extra cholesterol by reducing liver cholesterol production; for the rest, there is only a minor increase in cholesterol.

Which is good news for egg lovers, for eggs are cheap and contain the highest quality protein known. It is second only to mother's milk in terms of human nutrition and contains just 75 calories and 5 g (⅙ oz) of fat. Don't avoid the yolk for that is where the egg's vitamins and minerals are. And that makes an egg salad probably one of the best meal options to have if you're watching your weight and your budget. The trouble with such salads, however, is that most of them are creamy with mayonnaise; and if you're looking for an Asian egg salad, these are few and far between, except for this traditional recipe from Hunan.

Unusually, it marries the velvety richness of *peitan* or century eggs with the sweetness of roasted peppers or capsicums. A topping of raw chopped garlic adds a bite and everything is ameliorated with a dressing that is piquant and fragrant all at once. It is a terrific salad to serve as an appetiser, except that the preserved egg does reduce the nutritional value somewhat. However, its rich taste more than makes up for it while the coloured peppers up the antioxidant quotient. The chopped garlic, which has anti-bacterial properties, also make this dish one to eat for health.

Peitan, by the way, is only one of the several kinds of preserved egg. It is made by coating duck eggs in a paste made from mud, tea leaves, rice husks and salt together with alkaline ingredients such as wood ash, soda, lye and lime. The alkalis in this paste penetrate the shell and 'cook' the egg chemically. They change the texture and colour of the egg dramatically—the yolk turns soft and creamy while the white turns into a most appetizing amber gel. I love it, especially when it has a melting centre like ripe soft cheese, which to me is the only way to eat eggs, now that they have become respectable again.

Red capsicum (bell peppers) 3

Yellow capsicum (bell peppers) 3

Century eggs (*peitan*) 2, peeled and quartered

Chopped garlic 1–2 Tbsp

Light soy sauce 1 tsp

Rice vinegar 1 tsp, or more if you like it tart

Sesame oil 1 tsp

Washed baby spinach salad leaves 1 bag, or enough to line a salad plate

Salt to taste

Crushed black pepper to taste

1. Preheat oven to 200°C (400°F). Place whole capsicums on an oven tray and roast until blistered and blackened in parts.

2. While capsicums are roasting, scrape off the clay mixture from the shell of century eggs using a knife. Peel and cut into quarters. Leave for a while for the characteristic ammonia smell to dissipate.

3. Place capsicums in a plastic bag and loosely tie the bag, to make them sweat. This makes it easier to peel their skins later when they cool.

4. Slice capsicums into strips. Dress with chopped garlic, soy sauce, vinegar and sesame oil.

5. Place dressed capsicums on a bed of baby spinach leaves. Season with salt and pepper. Top with century egg quarters. Toss just before eating and watch how quickly this Chinese egg salad goes down!

serves 4

spring stir-fry

I used to turn up my nose at stir-fries—that familiar medley of vegetables, cooked perhaps with some slivers of meat or seafood. It was so traditional, it was boring. How blasé could I get? In truth, a stir-fry is possibly one of the healthiest ways to cook. Flash-fried, vegetables and meat cook quickly, retaining their goodness, while the medley of different vegetables ensures complete nutrition.

And if you choose seasonal vegetables, you get prime produce, securing sweetness and taste. Indeed all chefs know that if you cook with the best of seasonal foods, half the battle is won; you cannot help but create wonderful tastes. A stir-fry is also one of the easiest ways to cook a complete meal. Everything is cooked in one pan and in minutes. As for prep work, all it needs is cutting up of a handful of vegetables just before frying.

As for my prejudice about stir-fries—I got round it by going to the market without a shopping list. Instead, I allowed myself to be led by my eyes and picked out vegetables that were unusual. That day I found baby pumpkins from Japan, all the rage now that the cost had gone down and unusually also, some baby radishes, with leaves attached (the leaves can be eaten, by the way).

I also threw out notions of what a classic stir-fry should be and ended up with vegetables that were not usually found in such a medley. So aside from the pumpkins and the radishes, I included some fat asparagus. Theoretically, broad beans and peas are also in season. Sadly, these have to be obtained from the freezer, as none can be bought fresh here. Still, they are picked in the peak of condition and are flash-frozen.

This assortment became a Western stir-fry with a splash of white wine and topped with shavings of Parmesan cheese for a salty shot at the end. Try not to peel the vegetables as the most vitamins are in the skin. So I merely sliced the pumpkin into thin wedges but left the skin, which turned soft, tender and tasty after cooking. No longer will I label a stir-fry as boring again.

Young Japanese pumpkin 1

Young white radishes 4

Thick green asparagus spears 6

Frozen broad beans 1 cup

Extra virgin olive oil 2 Tbsp

Shallots 2, sliced

White wine 125 ml (4 fl oz / ½ cup)

Frozen baby peas 1 cup

Salt 1 tsp

Pepper to taste

Parmesan cheese a block for shaving

1. Slice pumpkin, skin and all, into thin wedges. Remove seeds using a teaspoon. Peel and slice baby radishes into 1-cm (½-in) thick pieces.

2. Peel ends of asparagus stems. Slice asparagus into 3-cm (1¼-in) lengths on the diagonal. Peel tough skin from broad beans.

3. Heat olive oil in a pan. When hot, add sliced shallots. Add pumpkin and radishes. Follow with white wine, and cook for about 5 minutes.

4. Add asparagus, the stems first, then the tips. Add peeled beans and baby peas.

5. Season with salt and pepper to taste. Dish out and finish with a swirl of extra virgin olive oil. Top with Parmesan cheese, shaved from the block with a potato peeler. Lovely with crusty bread.

serves 4

roast chicken and artichoke salad

Chicken breast is a great and healthy cut of meat—but it has few fans, because it is often dry and flavourless after cooking. Well, I have found a foolproof way making even lean meats such as chicken breast and pork loin moist and flavourful. You brine the meats before cooking.

The method is not really new—it came into prominence a few years ago when people started to brine turkeys before roasting them, in order to improve the taste of the unpopular though healthy meat. The problem with trying it out here is that our turkeys come frozen and ready brined (or at least injected with butter) and few of us have refrigerators large enough to accommodate a whole turkey for a couple of days, which is the length of time it takes to brine a big bird.

But a chicken breast is another proposition. So I tried it out with a simple solution of salt, sugar and water and roasted the breast afterwards. The results were amazing! The meat was moist and flavourful and did not really need the dressing that I had also prepared for the chicken.

What brining does is to deliver moisture and flavour right into the centre of the meat. According to Russ Parsons, who has written a fascinating book on the chemistry of cooking called *How to Read a French Fry*, the salt in the brine swells the meat fibres allowing the water to penetrate and to retain more of the water during cooking. Salt also seasons the meat not just on the surface, but right through. It is easy enough to attempt. All you need to do is to begin the preparation earlier. I brined the chicken breast for a couple of hours, but you can do it overnight or even days before, but be warned, the longer you brine, the saltier the meat will be, if you are concerned about ingesting too much salt.

As for the artichokes, which I served with the chicken, you could roast them yourself if you can find the small fresh ones on sale, but the bottled ones are delicious and convenient. The oil in which they are bottled also makes an extremely flavourful dressing. Added to the salad, they help to win back fans for chicken breast.

BRINE INGREDIENTS

Water 500 ml (16 fl oz / 2 cups)

Sugar 1 tsp

Salt 1 Tbsp

Bone-in chicken breasts 2

DRESSING

Artichoke olive oil (from bottled roasted artichokes)
250 ml (8 fl oz / 1 cup), top up with olive oil to make up amount

White wine vinegar 1 Tbsp

Salt a pinch

Sugar a pinch

Dijon mustard 1 tsp

SALAD INGREDIENTS

Butter lettuce 1 head

Rocket leaves a handful

Store-bought roasted artichokes in olive oil
about 8 heads, quartered

Tomatoes 2, quartered

Spring onion (scallion) 1, chopped

1. Prepare brine. Combine water, sugar and salt and stir. Place chicken breast in, cover and leave in the fridge overnight or for at least 2 hours.

2. Heat oven 200°C (400°F). Remove chicken from brine and pat dry. Prepare dressing by combining all ingredients. Coat chicken breasts with dressing.

3. Heat a frying pan over medium heat. Without adding any oil, quickly brown chicken breasts. Remove and place on a baking tray, then place in oven to cook for 10 minutes. If juices run clear when chicken is pierced with the tip of a knife, it is cooked. Remove from oven and leave aside for 5 minutes.

4. Make up salad with butter lettuce and rocket leaves. Slice chicken, and together with artichokes, place on bed of salad leaves. Garnish with tomatoes and spring onion. Pour over remaining salad dressing and serve.

serves 3-4

thai roasted eggplant salad with soft-centred eggs

If you're bored with salads, don't be. The hot weather means that we are eating salads more often then ever in my household. And we look for main course salads that can be consumed as a meal, cutting down on the calories even more. *Yum*, or a Thai salad is a good option, provided you up the protein component to make it nutritionally complete. Thai salads have little oil and yet are tasty with fish sauce, sweet with onion and piquant with chilli and lime juice.

Unfortunately, most of these fresh salads are also enriched by liberal amounts of cholesterol-rich dried prawns or as in the famed Thai catfish salad, with a crispy topping of flaked catfish that is battered, then deep-fried. I ignore such steps (the oil and the mess!) Instead, I have substituted packaged fish floss when this topping is called for. This you can buy from those roasted pork (*bak kua*) stalls and they even offer a crispy version if you like crunch. Just remember they are already sweetened, so hold back on the sugar.

The eggplants have to be the slim purple or green Asian eggplants as they are not bitter and become sweet and soft upon being roasted. Remember their juices will make up part of the dressing. And, of course, they have to be roasted to get that irresistible smokiness. The eggs also have to be boiled just so to get a soft yielding centre, which add their own creamy finish to the salad. But once you get these two steps right, it takes mere assembly to compose this full-course salad. Now for the eggplant itself. Though it is part of the dreaded nightshade family (which includes peppers, potatoes and tomatoes) and should be avoided by those suffering from arthritis and related problems of the bones and joints, for the rest of us the benefits are many.

Eggplant has ample bioflavonoids, which may be beneficial in preventing strokes and hemorrhages. The fruit also contains antioxidants helpful in preventing heart disease and cancer. And we are not even mentioning the protein and other good things found in eggs and even the fish floss. Something to chew upon when I am eating this full-flavoured salad!

Long purple and/or green eggplants (aubergines/brinjals) 4

Eggs 2–4 (depending on individual preference)

Cucumber 1, sliced

Shallots 4, peeled and sliced

Red chillies 2, sliced

Lime juice 2 Tbsp

Fish sauce 1 Tbsp

Fresh herbs like coriander, mint and basil leaves (optional) a handful, chopped

Crispy fish floss

1. Place whole eggplants under the grill and cook until charred and soft. Transfer to a plastic bag, seal with a rubber band and leave to steam. The eggplants will peel easily once cooled.

2. Place eggs in a pot and cover with cold water. Bring to the boil and turn off heat. Leave eggs submerged in hot water for 5 minutes, then drain and add cold water to arrest the cooking. This will ensure the yolks remain soft and melting. Leave aside until later.

3. When eggplants have cooled, peel and cut into pieces. Place on a plate. Scatter sliced cucumber, shallots and chillies over. Add lime juice and fish sauce and toss to combine.

4. Peel eggs and cut into half. Arrange on the salad plate on top of the dressed eggplants. Add a pinch of salt on each of the egg halves.

5. If using, scatter chopped herbs and add about 1 Tbsp fish floss over everything just before serving. It will add sweet crunch to the salad. *Yum* indeed!

serves 4

spinach and tofu towers

Spinach and soy bean curd are so healthful that one does not associate high style with these foods. Yet the Chinese restaurants have worked wonders with these everyday ingredients.

They have created tasty appetisers that look so stylish that one forgets their nutritional benefits. Here the two ingredients have been cooked lightly, chopped and combined to make a mixture that is then formed into little towers for the appetizer plate. It is a great presentation that makes one forget its prosaic health benefits, though there are many.

Spinach is free of saturated fat, cholesterol and is low in calories. It is also a good source of fibre, vitamins A and C, iron, folate and magnesium. Similarly soy bean curd, in all its various forms, is a good source of high-quality protein (especially for vegetarians), vitamin B and iron. Moreover, it is touted to have anti-carcinogenic, antioxidant and cholesterol-lowering properties.

While there is some controversy surrounding soy's health benefits, I always say that it is an ancient food that has been eaten by the Chinese for centuries without ill-effect. As with all things, moderation is the key.

The recipe is unbelievably simple. When I first ate it at a Chinese restaurant, it was featured as a cold appetiser and came in a pyramid-shaped tower. How dramatic! Having eaten spinach and *tau kwa* (firm bean curd) in all manner of recipes and presentations, this one was novel and truly tasty. Yet I was intrigued at how easy it was to replicate. All you needed to do was to cook the spinach and chop it fine before mixing it with the finely diced *tau kwa* and—this is the secret—packing it tightly into small containers.

I used a small glass bowl that I filled to the brim, an important point for you do not want the concoction to fall apart when you unmould it. There are other advantages to this dish. It is easy to make, needing less than half an hour of preparation and can be done ahead of time, easy if you're entertaining.

Me, I am just happy to find yet one more spinach and soy bean recipe for my collection!

English or Chinese spinach 400 g (14⅓ oz)

Firm bean curd (*tau kwa*) 2 cakes

Salt a pinch

Sesame oil 1 tsp

Sugar ½ tsp

Light soy sauce ½ tsp

Ground white pepper to taste

1. Wash spinach thoroughly to rid it of dirt and soak in cold water for 30 minutes to revive the leaves. Drain well.

2. Bring a pot of water to boil. Cook spinach for a few minutes, just to soften. Rinse under a cold tap for a few minutes to arrest the cooking, then squeeze leaves dry. Chop finely and leave aside.

3. Heat 1 tsp cooking oil in a small pan and lightly fry bean curd cakes. Remove and cut into small dice. Leave to cool.

4. Combine spinach and bean curd pieces in a bowl. Season with salt, sesame oil, sugar and soy sauce. Add pepper to taste.

5. Pack this mixture tightly into four small bowls, filling to the brim (I used cone-shaped dessert bowls). Cover bowls with plastic wrap and leave in the fridge to chill and set.

6. Just before serving, unmould spinach and bean curd cones. Place a plate that you want to serve the appetiser on over the bowl and upturn it. A tap on the bottom of the bowl should loosen the cone.

serves 4-5

peppered crabmeat salad

If you're worried about that mound of crabmeat in the middle of this salad, don't be.

Interestingly, the Japanese believe that cholesterol from seafood is less harmful than that from meat, because seafood has less fat, making it more acceptable for those watching their cholesterol levels.

In fact, the cholesterol levels found in most seafood are about the same as that of meat. And despite its bad reputation, the cholesterol count for crab is just about 42 mg for every 100 g (3½ oz) as compared with healthy salmon's 39 mg. To compare, prawn (shrimp) is about 70 mg.

Plus to put it into perspective, a cup of crabmeat is here shared among 4–5 persons.

Here it is seasoned with black pepper, garlic and coriander root, a Thai classic seasoning for crab, and it delivers a potent punch. Moreover, there is no added oil except for the spoonful used to dress the salad leaves. A squeeze of lemon juice helps to cut through any satiety.

Crushed black pepper 2 Tbsp

Coriander (cilantro) roots 6–8

Garlic 2 cloves

Pasteurised crabmeat 220 g (8 oz), available from supermarkets or use fresh crabmeat

Salt a pinch

Butter lettuce 1 head

Red butter lettuce I head

Sea salt ½ tsp

Lemon ½, squeezed for juice

Extra virgin olive oil 1 Tbsp

Cherry tomatoes 5–6, halved

1. Pound pepper, coriander root and garlic together until fine. Place crabmeat in a bowl and add the pounded seasoning. Mix to combine. Add salt. Pack dressed crabmeat into a round ring, available from cookware shops.

2. Cut off the hard stems at the bottom of each head of lettuce. Detach the leaves. Wash and drain, then tear into smaller sizes. Place in a bowl and season with salt. Dress with lemon juice and olive oil. Toss well.

3. Place dressed leaves on a plate and unmould crabmeat on top. Scatter cherry tomato halves to decorate. Serve chilled either on its own with toast tips, or as a part of a meal.

serves 4-5

crabmeat and mango rice paper rolls

We cannot have too many ways to eat a salad.

With the injunction to eat fruits and vegetables at least 5 times a day, I look for as many different ways to eat my greens as I can. And if they are raw, all the better, for the vitamins would be better preserved.

While we do not have many salad eating options in Singapore, the Nyonya *kueh pie tee* could be described as a salad (or rather vegetables) in a cup while the *poh piah* is but a vegetable roll. While the vegetables are cooked in these cases, there is nothing to stop one from making a raw version. I did one with *pie tee* shells the other day using a raw green mango salad as filling. It was refreshing and satisfying, thanks to the fried flour cup, which unfortunately moves that recipe out of the healthy range.

For imaginative and healthy salad options, look to Vietnamese cuisine. Sometimes, their pomelo or banana flower salads come on a crisp rice cracker; sometimes, they wrap their greens in rice paper. Called *goi cuon*, this fresh roll usually comprises pork, prawn, wrapped together with lettuce, herbs and rice vermicelli in rice paper. Taking that idea further, I do versions of it depending on what I have in the fridge. So it could be avocado and crab, carrot and cucumber sticks with chopped nuts, or prawn and radish sprouts.

These rolls need no real cooking, are convenient to eat and lovely to look at if you add some colour, which could come from a carrot, a chilli or a mango, as in this case. The rice paper sheet makes an excellent wrap as it is quite hardy and yet delicate so it does not sit heavy in the stomach. In Vietnam, you can get several varieties of rice papers of different thicknesses, but the most easily available outside the country are the dried rounds, measuring about 17 cm (6½ in) in diameter. They are obtainable from the dried food section in the supermarkets.

While many recipes advise dampening the rice paper with a wet towel, you need not do this. I find that the moisture in the leaves themselves softens the paper sufficiently for rolling. All done, there is nothing like a chilled parcel of crisp crunch, dunked into a savoury nut sauce to hit the spot, especially when the weather's hot. A chilled salad roll is indeed a perfect delivery system for eating greens.

Dried rice paper rounds 8–10 pieces, about 17 cm (6½ in) in diameter

Butter lettuce leaves 4, hard stems flattened and torn into half

Cucumber ½, shredded coarsely

Fresh herbs (mint and sweet basil leaves)

Coriander (cilantro) leaves 1 bunch, separated into sprigs

Crabmeat 1 cup

Mango ½, peeled and sliced into thick slivers

DIPPING SAUCE

Roasted peeled almonds 1 cup, chopped finely

Garlic 2 cloves, chopped fine

Red chilli 1, chopped fine

Lemon grass 1 stalk, ends trimmed, hard outer leaves removed and chopped finely

Fish sauce 1 tsp or to taste

Sugar 1 Tbsp or to taste

Lime juice 1 Tbsp or to taste

1. Lay a rice paper round on a flat plate. Line it with a lettuce leaf to help hold the ingredients better. Top with shredded cucumber and fresh herbs, including a sprig of coriander. Add a dollop of crabmeat.

2. By this time, the greens would have softened the dried rice paper a little. You should be able to roll it up into a cone, encasing the filling snugly.

3. Tuck in a mango sliver at the open end of the roll. Repeat for the other rolls. You should have enough to make 8 rolls altogether.

4. Place in the fridge, covered with plastic wrap, to chill. Meanwhile, prepare dipping sauce by blending all ingredients in a food processor. Serve rolls chilled, together with dipping sauce.

serves 4

steamed tofu custard with crispy white bait

A meal entirely based on bean curd. Only the Japanese could do this, and successfully, too. They have tofu restaurants in the country where several courses are designed round the soy bean and its many products. Such a meal is subtle, light and comforting.

In it, you may get plain tofu, cold and hot, served with a sauce, followed by perhaps grilled tofu (served with a smear of different flavours of miso) and simmered tofu or *yudoufu*, cooked with yam and perhaps fish. They even use the tofu skin—what they call *yuba* and what we call *fu chok*—which they once served fresh on ice with a delicious onion dip. But despite their many ways with tofu, I have never come across it steamed in a custard.

That seems to be the Chinese way, though the Japanese do have *chawan mushi*, a custard soup cooked plain or with seafood, chicken or vegetables. The Chinese repertoire of savoury custards includes one topped with *mee sua* (wheat vermicelli) noodles or with seafood, a prawn or even a half a crayfish. We are also familiar with that family favourite of steamed three kinds of egg—fresh, salted and preserved. It has to be quivery, soft and silky, a true test of cooking skills.

This recipe below is a take on all these beloved dishes, plus tofu, which gives us yet another way to eat this healthy soy bean product. Another difference—it uses egg white in the custard, upping further the health quotient. Yet it is no less tasty; the custard is topped here with umami-rich crispy white bait plus a swirl of its fragrant oil, ensuring that every bit of tofu and egg will be scraped out from the bowl! Aside from its widely known health benefits, this is an extremely versatile dish for it can served both as an appetiser when entertaining and as an everyday dish.

To ensure a silky and smooth custard, the proportion of liquid to egg is important, as is the timing of the cooking. Here I've timed it for just 10 minutes but over a medium fire to ensure that the custard sets just so.

TOPPING

Dried white bait 1 tsp

Vegetable oil 2 Tbsp

CUSTARD

Egg whites 2

Chicken stock or water 250 ml (4 fl oz / 1 cup)

Rice wine 1 tsp

Sugar a pinch

Salt ½ tsp (if using water or unsalted stock)

Round white or egg tofu 2 thick slices

1. Rinse white bait and dry well using kitchen paper.

2. Heat oil in a frying pan over low heat. Fry white bait until crisp, stirring all the time to ensure it does not burn.

3. Remove both crisped fish and oil. Place in separate containers for use later.

4. Fill a wok up to halfway with water and bring to the boil.

5. Meanwhile, separate egg whites and yolks. Leave yolks aside for another use. In a bowl, stir egg whites and chicken stock or water. Add rice wine, sugar and salt, if needed, to season.

6. Place tofu slices in a small heatproof bowl, cup or ramekin. Pour custard mixture over.

7. The water in the wok should now be simmering. Steam custard, with wok covered, for 10 minutes or until just set. Top with crisp white bait and a swirl of its oil. Serve at once.

serves 4-5

roasted pumpkin and pickled onion salad

Christmas is over, but Chinese New Year beckons. The feasting never seems to end, especially at this time. We have scarcely a month to pare down before we feast yet again. And plant foods, or salads, are still the way to go, if one wants to watch the calories.

The trouble with a salad is that it is, well, rabbit food, as some would put it. They dislike it for the precise reasons why I like it—its crunch, its lightness on the stomach and its green tastes.So for those who hate their salads green but still want to opt for such meals to prepare for the inevitable feasting ahead, I have this roasted pumpkin salad that is as full-bodied as it is healthy.

I serve it often for lunch and love the sweet caramelization that roasting brings out from the vegetable or more strictly, fruit. To cut the sweetness, I top the roasted vegetable with raw onions that have been pickled and fresh green chillies for some bite.

Butternut is not strictly a pumpkin but a squash, though it is known as a pumpkin in Australia and is treated as such (squash and its many varieties originate from Mexico, while pumpkins come from South America). Whatever, butternut is the sweetest of that family of vegetables so you can rest assured when you choose it over the other varieties. You could also allow the pumpkin to ripen first before using it, leaving it out in a cool dark place and only using it after a few days. Less known is the fact that pumpkin is a good source of fibre, vitamin C, manganese, magnesium, and potassium and also an excellent source of vitamin A.

In cooking terms, it is lovely in soups, braises, grills or even stir-fries. Indeed, one of my favourite pumpkin stir-fries is to top it with crunchy bits of salted fish to give a salty bite to the sweet vegetable. Another way is to add balsamic vinegar to roasted pumpkin and top it with crumbled ricotta cheese and some torn basil leaves. For pumpkin with Thai flavours, I use fish sauce instead of salt as seasoning and finish off with a scattering of roasted peanuts and toasted dried shrimp on top.

And there you have it, salad options that are full of rich, moreish flavours and yet, still a salad.

Red onion 1

Lemon ½, squeezed for juice

Medium-sized butternut squash 1, about 1 kg (2 lb 3 oz)

Olive oil 2 Tbsp

Cherry tomatoes 12

Salt 1 tsp

Pepper to taste

Green chillies 2

1. Preheat oven to 200°C (400°F).

2. Peel and slice onion. Pour lemon juice over the sliced onions. Add a pinch of salt to season and leave aside.

3. Cut butternut squash into half and peel using a potato peeler. If this proves difficult, soften the gourd by microwaving on High for a few minutes.

4. Cut squash into 2.5-cm (1-in) square cubes. Add olive oil, salt, pepper and toss to coat. Place marinated squash and cherry tomatoes on a baking tray and roast for 30 minutes or until caramelised and burnt in parts.

5. To serve, place roasted pumpkin and tomatoes on a bed of lettuce leaves, top with pickled onion rings and its juice, and sliced green chillies. Add a swirl of olive oil to finish.

serves 4

meat and poultry

meats

don't forget meat in a healthy diet.
despite popular misgivings about eating
meat, especially red meat, it plays an
important part in a balanced diet.

meat provides protein, which is important
for muscle building and repair, and is
a good source of iron and zinc. besides,
it just tastes good! just be sure to choose
the leaner cuts and a healthier way of
cooking them.

meats

asian pork terrine

Poor pork. It has been seriously misunderstood. Although a white meat, it has been wrongly labelled as unhealthy and 'dirty' which is why so many diets forbid consumption of the meat.

It is not surprising though. For years, pork has been the source of trichinosis, a disease caused by a bacteria particular to infected meat, killed only by high cooking temperatures. And yet a restaurant called Blue Hill at Stone Barns in the Hudson Valley outside New York City, serves pink pork to its diners. Yes, pink! Deliciously juicy and underdone, the waiter explained that theirs was organic pork obtained from their own pigs, fed only on apples and hay, making their meat clean as a whistle. It was a sweet taste of pork that I had long forgotten.

Indeed with modern breeding practices, trichinosis is no longer a problem and even if it is, trichina (the bacteria) is killed at 70°C (158°F), well below the usual cooking temperatures for pork. Besides, there are other reasons to choose pork. The tenderloin or fillet for example has lower cholesterol than even skinless chicken breast. Pork also has lots of minerals and in particular, thiamin, which helps to metabolise carbohydrate, protein and fat.

It is undisputedly an indispensable part of a healthy diet and even if it isn't, the Chinese are genetically predisposed to eating pork, according to a friend's mad theory. He may well say that of the Germans, English, Italians and yes, the Vietnamese. If you visit Ho Chi Minh City, you can find street stalls selling a pork terrine stuffed into bagettes, the French's contribution to that country's cuisine. This terrine is terrific. It is cooked with lots of Vietnamese herbs and eaten with yet more fresh greens. Seasoned with fish sauce, it delivers an Asian punch to a Western-style meat loaf.

Here I use only lean pork, crunchy black fungus and fresh herbs. A couple of red chillies give colour and a salve of sweet mustard perks up the final mouthful.

TERRINE

Lean pork mince 500 g (1 lb 1½ oz)

Red onion 1, peeled and chopped finely

Garlic 2 cloves, peeled and chopped finely

Basil, mint, laksa and coriander (cilantro) leaves
A small bunch of each, washed well and finely chopped

Large red chillies 2, chopped

Dried black fungus 4–5 pieces, soaked to soften, then drained and chopped

Egg 1

Salt to taste

Fish sauce 1 tsp or to taste

Ground white pepper to taste

TO SERVE

Small hamburger buns 8–10

Green and red chillies (optional)

Lettuce leaves

Basil, mint or coriander (cilantro) leaves

Sweet mustard (add sugar and vinegar to taste to store-bought wholegrain mustard)

1. Preheat oven to 160°C (325°F). Prepare terrine. Place pork mince in a large basin. Add chopped onion, garlic, chopped herbs, chilli, black fungus and egg. Season with salt, fish sauce and white pepper. Mix well and set aside.

2. Grease the inside of a loaf tin or similar bakeware and pack filling tightly into the tin. Cover meat with a piece of foil to keep it moist during cooking. Place loaf tin in an oven tray and pour enough water into the tray to come up to half the sides of the tin. This ensures gentle cooking.

3. Place in oven to cook for 30 minutes. Poke terrine with a skewer to check that the juices runs clear, an indication that it is cooked. Remove from oven and leave to cool. Run a knife round the edges and upturn the terrine onto a plate. Slice.

4. To serve, place a slice into a halved bun. Add lettuce leaves, herbs and chillies, if liked. Add a smear of mustard and you've got a delicious (and healthy) Asian sandwich in your hands.

serves 8-10

ayam tempra

Squeeze lime juice over any dish and straightaway the flavours come alive. The Peranakans knew that. So many of their dishes call for a squirt of lime just before serving. Where would *mee rebus* or *mee siam* be without that sour finish? Not many people know, however, that the Peranakans also have a stir-fried chicken dish where lime juice lifts the soy sauce gravy to mouthwatering heights. I am talking about the Nyonya classic—*ayam tempra*, or chicken with a lime-spiked soy sauce. It is a dish with a history, for this idea of marinating meats in lime juice (or vinegar) probably stemmed from the Portuguese who long ago lived in these parts and had a habit of curing meats in this manner.

Despite it being rooted in tradition, ayam tempra has very updated characteristics. It uses lean meat chicken breast, in this case, but I remember my grandmother also relying on the same recipe for fish or lean pork. And you could reduce the fat even further by stripping the skin off the breast. Second, the sautéed chicken relies only on soy sauce and lime juice for taste. Not much fat and certainly no coconut. Quite rare for an old recipe. It is an easy dish to turn out, taking just minutes, if you rely on those packs of chicken breast now available from the supermarkets.

The dish relies on lime flavours for a lift. And limes are a wonderful ingredient, both for its floral scent and for health. The fruit is rich in Vitamin C and dietary fibre. It also contains anti-inflammatory nutrients—Vitamin C, of course, folate and beta carotene. All parts of the fruit can be used. Not just the juice, but also the leaves and the lime zest to up the limey flavours. A natural flavour enhancer, I like to use it instead of vinegar in my salad dressings, squeeze a bit into sauces and soups or add it to marinades. I try to use the old-fashioned marble-sized deep green *limau kesturi*, or calamansi limes for this dish, but you could substitute with other kinds of limes instead.

Whichever, they should be shiny, be deep-green in colour, feel heavy for their size and have a thin smooth skin. With such qualities, you can be assured of lots of juice inside. If you are using the bigger limes (or Indian limes), just roll them, pressing down on the counter to release the juices before squeezing.

Vegetable oil 2 Tbsp

Large red onion 1, peeled and sliced

Chicken breasts 4, sliced thickly

Dark soy sauce 1 Tbsp

Salt ½ tsp

Sugar 1 Tbsp

Water 125 ml (4 fl oz / ½ cup)

Red chillies 2, sliced

Calamansi limes (*limau kesturi*) 4 or to taste, squeezed for juice

Kaffir lime leaves for garnish

1. Heat oil in a wok over medium heat and fry onions until soft and browned. This will sweeten the dish.

2. Brown chicken pieces. Season with soy sauce, salt and sugar. Allow to caramelize, then pour water over the meat to deglaze the pan, that is, to obtain a sauce from the pan juices.

3. When chicken is tender, add the chillies and squeeze lime juice over just before serving. If liked, garnish with kaffir lime leaves or shredded lime peel for extra fragrance.

4. Serve with plain rice.

spice-rubbed roasted beef fillet

In the bad old days when red meat was regularly left out in the cold by the health-conscious, I remember a meal I once cooked for a teenager. She took one look at the table and asked: where's the beef? Of course, it was not there. I had taken it off my list of safe foods, simply because I had thought, wrongly, that red meat is to be avoided at all costs. As it turns out, red meat has been unfairly maligned.

Few know that beef, for example, can be included in a low-fat diet and that it gives more nutrition, calorie for calorie, than a similar piece of chicken! It has eight times more vitamin B12, six times more zinc and three times more iron than a similar-sized piece of chicken breast.

Fewer even realise that it can play a role in a cholesterol-lowering diet. Beef has only 1.2 g of fat more than a skinless chicken breast, and indeed less fat than a skinless chicken leg, for those of you who like dark meat. And the way to continue to eating red meat is to choose your cut properly.

In fact, I now enjoy beef and lamb at least once a week. And I can do this, because I choose only the lean cuts like the fillet, flank or the eye round to cook. Their saturated fat content ranges from 1.4–2.7 g for every 85 g serving.

And while I love marbled meat such as the rib eye, onglet and prime rib for their flavour, I have now learnt to add more taste to lean meat by marinating it first and then serving it with a piquant sauce.

I chose a Mexican spice rub simply because I like the fresh tomato salsa that is a traditional match. I then added browned onions (sliced onions fried in olive oil and seasoned with a pinch of salt) to ensure even more zing.

Valuable taste tips now that we know that healthy eating does not mean eschewing red meat from the diet.

Beef fillet 450 g (16 oz)

Chilli powder 1 tsp

Cumin powder 1 tsp

Paprika powder 1 tsp

Salt 1 tsp

Crushed black pepper ½ tsp

Extra virgin olive oil 2 Tbsp

TOMATO SALSA (MAKES ONE LARGE BOWL)

Ripe tomatoes 4, chopped

Onions ½, peeled and chopped

Coriander (cilantro) leaves ½ cup, chopped

Green chillies 4, chopped

Juice from half a lemon or to taste

Sugar 1 tsp

Salt ½ tsp

1. Prepare tomato salsa a few hours in advance. Place vegetables in a bowl and season with lemon juice, salt and sugar. Stir well to combine and leave chilled in the fridge for flavours to meld together.

2. Pat dry beef fillet with paper towels and rub powdered spices well into the meat, followed by salt and pepper.

3. Drizzle with olive oil. Cover with plastic wrap and leave in the fridge for a couple of hours to marinate.

4. When ready to cook, preheat oven to 200°C (400°F). Place baking rack in the middle. Heat a pan over medium heat until hot. Sear seasoned fillet a couple of minutes on each side to seal the meat.

5. Place browned meat in the middle of an oven pan and roast for 10 minutes for medium-rare meat. Remove from oven to rest for 5 minutes, then slice into 8–9 steaks, about 2–3 cm (1–1½-in) thick.

6. Divide steaks among prepared serving plates and keeping to the Mexican theme, serve with tomato salsa and browned onions on the side.

serves 4-5

mushrooms and black fungus with seared flank steak

I don't know if you have noticed, but we have some new and truly beautiful varieties of mushrooms on the supermarket shelves. They come in luscious shades of coffee, suede and cream, some clumped together like a flower, others like a clutch of pretty round buttons. For years, we had to settle for just canned button mushrooms and dried shiitakes or Chinese mushrooms, then came the white buttons, the first fresh mushrooms in the market. These days, we have more, much more.

There are brown creminis and large portobellos that look like flying saucers, different varieties of oyster mushrooms, with thick succulent stems that taste really meaty, tiny baby enokis, and the velvety shimeji mushrooms. The best thing about them is that they are fresh, being grown locally so they arrive on the shelves quicker than imported mushrooms, which take more than a week to arrive. And as any cook will tell you, the shorter time from the farm to the pot will result in better flavour and nutrition from the product.

If you do not already know, mushrooms are a rich source of proteins and vitamins (B, C, D), minerals (phosphates and potassium) and fibre. Mushrooms also have therapeutic properties that trigger off the body's immune system. And of course they are truly delicious since they contain huge amounts of the fifth taste, identified by the Japanese as umami. I could not resist these new varieties of mushrooms. I decided to sauté them and pile them over slices of rare beef. Instead of steak and mushrooms, we would have mushrooms and steak!

For those of you who are still avoiding red meat, flank steak is fine because it is lean. Indeed its fat content is less than that of a skinless chicken thigh. Anyway, we are talking of only a few slices of beef per person here, loading up instead with mushrooms.

The combination of steak and mushrooms is classic and is especially delicious here, lifted by a splash of rice wine and black vinegar. A dusting of chilli gives some bite. And to think it started out with me being tantalized by those displays of beautiful mushrooms.

Mixed fresh mushrooms (such as king oyster, baby enoki, willow and brown shimeji), or preferred combination 400 g (14$\frac{1}{3}$ oz)

Dried black fungus 4–5 pieces, reconstituted in water for 30 minutes

Flank steak 600 g (1 lb 5$\frac{1}{3}$ oz), cut into 2 pieces

Salt a pinch

Crushed black pepper to taste

Olive oil 2 Tbsp

Onions 2, peeled and sliced

Garlic 2 cloves, minced

Dried chilli flakes ½ tsp

Rice wine 1 Tbsp

Black vinegar 1 Tbsp

1. Prepare mushrooms by wiping them with a damp towel. Do not rinse nor soak them as they will turn soggy. Cut off the hard bottoms of the stems, then slice them, if large, and separate the smaller mushrooms that are in a bunch. Drain softened black fungus and set aside.

2. Pat dry steaks with a paper towel, then rub salt and pepper over them. In a grill pan, heat 1 Tbsp olive oil over medium-high heat. Cook steaks for 2 minutes on each side if you want steaks rare, or 3–4 minutes for medium doneness. Remove from heat and set aside.

3. Heat remaining oil in a frying pan. Brown onions and garlic until softened, then add mushrooms, starting with the king oyster mushrooms. Add black fungus and season with chilli flakes and a bit of salt and pepper to taste. After a few minutes, add rice wine and black vinegar. Toss well to mix and fry for a few more minutes until mushrooms soften.

4. Slice steak into smaller pieces across the grain and place on a serving plate. Pile on the mushrooms together with the pan juices. Serve with rice, noodles, pasta or mashed potato.

serves 4-6

seared lamb loin in a herb broth

It was red meat but it was healthful—just pieces of lean lamb bathed in a clear herb-flavoured broth, surrounded by tender baby vegetables.

When I first ate a version of this dish at a French restaurant, I was thrilled! Unlike the rich wine sauces that usually finish off a red meat dish, the meat here sat in a clean broth. If you are a follower of cooking programmes (like I am), you will know that most red wine sauces are finished off with a dollop of pure butter, added to emulsify the gravy, enriching the flavour and thickening the sauce.

But the lamb I ordered at this restaurant was different in so many ways. The meat was cut small, in slices that were not as off-putting as those monster steaks. The broth in which the meat came was clear (no butter here) and the accompanying baby vegetables were as lightly cooked as a Chinese stir-fry, another surprise.

I resolved to attempt a recipe at home so that I could add it to my store of healthy meat dishes, quite hard to find as the health-conscious would attest to. And I am happy to report that it turned out a success. I now love this lamb dish, so much that I am buying up lamb fillets every time they are on offer so that I can cook it yet one more time! For those who do not know, the tenderloin of the animal, from where the fillet steak is cut, offers lean and tender meat.

If you love lamb, you will like this dish where the sweet taste of lamb is not overwhelmed by heavy sauces or gravies. The cooking takes little time, just a gentle sear in a hot pan, then a gentle poaching in a broth, which could be just water or vegetable stock to begin with. As you add the other ingredients, they will give layers of flavour to what is essentially a clear stock.

For those still unconvinced of the benefits of eating lamb, 100 g of lean lamb will give you 25 per cent of your daily protein requirements, your essential amino acids, less then 6 g of saturated fat, less than 50 mg of cholesterol and a good supply of B vitamins, iron and zinc. The fibre and vitamin C come from the accompanying vegetables. So there you are, all your vitamin needs in one dish, albeit red meat!

LEMON MINT SAUCE

Fresh mint leaves 1 cup

Lemon ½, squeezed for juice

Salt a pinch

Extra virgin olive oil

LAMB

Lamb tenderloin 1, about 500 g (1 lb 1½ oz), fat trimmed

Salt to taste

Crushed black pepper to taste

HERB BROTH

Unsalted vegetable stock or water 1 litre (32 fl oz / 4 cups)

White wine 125 ml (4 fl oz / ½ cup)

A selection of vegetables (young potatoes, baby carrots, baby corn and fine green beans) 2 each for potatoes, carrots and baby corn and a handful of green beans for each person, cut into equal sizes

1. Prepare lemon mint sauce. Chop finely mint leaves. Place in a bowl and add lemon juice, salt and enough olive oil to cover ingredients. Mix well and leave aside for flavours to amalgamate.

2. Season lamb with salt and pepper to taste. Heat grill pan until hot, then sear all sides of the meat until browned and caramelised. Remove and leave aside.

3. Prepare herb broth. Bring vegetable stock or water to boil. Place vegetables in and poach gently until carrots are tender. Add white wine and season with salt and pepper to taste.

4. Remove vegetables and set aside. Return stock to the boil again and poach lamb gently for about 10 minutes. Add a dollop of lemon mint sauce, then remove meat and leave aside for another 10 minutes. Keep broth warm.

5. Slice meat and divide among 4 plates. Divide vegetables equally and ladle broth over. Spoon lemon mint sauce on top of meat and serve.

serves 4

vietnamese chicken satay

Think of a cooking method that just melts away the fat, leaving behind lots of succulent flavour.

That's grilling, a too-often overlooked and yet ideal way of cooking meats and vegetables. Not only that, grilled foods offer a simplicity of taste, ideal for post-festive periods when our palates have been assaulted by too many sauces and flavours.

Grilled vegetables taste sweeter and even fruit like pineapple and pears achieve a rich caramelisation when grilled. While I hanker after grilled meats on occasion, I like them well marinated and in bite-sized pieces. Satay suits the bill, but I like a Vietnamese satay, where the seasonings are lighter. Vietnamese satay is fragrant with lemon grass and the chicken pieces are threaded on a skewer, interspersed with young calamansi lime (*limau kesturi*) leaves, turning up the lemon/lime factor to the max!

Aside from its fragrance, lemon grass is also a good source of folate, magnesium, zinc and copper, and a very good source of iron, potassium and manganese. It also has anti-inflammatory properties. The bush may look like an overgrown clump of *lallang*, but you want not the leaves, but the white bulbous stems at the base which when sliced, reveal bands of colour between the layers. This is where the fragrance resides.

As with Malay satay, onions and garlic form the bulk of the marinade, together with salt, pepper and sugar. Instead of the trade spices of cumin and coriander found in satay, the Vietnamese grilled chicken relies on turmeric, lemon grass, ginger and the inevitable fish sauce for flavouring.

No worries about making the spice paste, a food processor does the job in minutes. Here, I use boneless chicken—it is easier to cook, taking just minutes on each side to obtain flavourful meat.

SPICE PASTE

Lemon grass 2 stalks, ends trimmed, hard outer leaves removed and cut into short lengths

Garlic 2 cloves, peeled

Shallots 4

Turmeric powder 1 tsp

Ginger 1 thumb-size knob ,peeled

Vegetable oil 2 Tbsp

Fish sauce 1 tsp

Salt 1 tsp

Pepper to taste

Sugar 1 tsp

SATAY

Dark chicken meat 200 g (7 oz), skin and visible fat removed and cut into small pieces

Young calamansi lime (*limau kesturi*) leaves 20

Bamboo skewers 10, soaked in water for 15 minutes before use

1. Prepare spice paste. Combine ingredients except seasonings in a food processor and pulse until fine. Add fish sauce, salt, pepper and sugar, sparingly because you do not want the chicken to burn.

2. Rub paste well into the meat. Leave covered in the fridge overnight or for at least 2 hours.

3. Thread 2–3 chicken pieces each onto soaked bamboo skewers, interspersing with lime leaves. Spread remaining marinade over the skewered meat.

4. Grill over a medium fire or heat on the barbecue, or under the grill, turning often to ensure even browning. Serve immediately.

Tip: Lemon grass stems make good basters. Just bruise the bulbs until they fan out, then dip them into oil to use as brushes over the grilled items.

serves 2-3

steamed beef with chinese cabbage

Not only is there beefy goodness in this dish, it is wholesome eating and takes just 15 minutes to turn out. It is thin slices of beef, cooked by steaming, a cooking method long neglected, especially for meats. And it needs no added oil, yet retains the juiciness and all the flavour of the meat, even if it is a lean cut such as the tenderloin. I first ate beef cooked this way at a sushi restaurant, where they used thin slices of well-marbled wagyu beef. But what if I substituted the marbled cut for a lean one?

It worked. The trick lay in the marinating and in the timing. You need to marinate the meat for a few hours at least, if not overnight, in a light rice wine and soy sauce marinade and cook it for just 10 minutes. The result is tender and tasty meat overlaid with the sweetness of Chinese cabbage, also known as Napa cabbage.

It is also low carbohydrate eating which is all the rage these days and yet makes for a satisfying meal with both meat and vegetable on the plate. To make it even more convenient, both vegetables and meat are cooked together in one of those bamboo dim-sum baskets, which practically every household has. The meat is laid directly on the rack at the bottom of the basket, allowing the steam to penetrate directly into the meat.

I served this lightly cooked beef with a lemon-infused soy sauce, dressed with thinly sliced red chilli and spring onion, and it is sensational eating. Lean beef is an often overlooked cut of meat especially in these days of eating white meat and fish, and yet it is a superior source of protein and B vitamins.

To put it into perspective, one serving of lean beef contains just 168 calories and 4.6 g of fat (including 1.7 g of saturated fat) compared with a similar serving of skinless, chicken breast which has 169 calories and 3 g of fats including 1 g of saturated fat. In fact, there are 19 cuts of lean beef, of which the round steak tops the list. The flank, tenderloin and the sirloin (trimmed of its characteristic strip of fat) are included in this group. But generally, you can anyway see if a piece of meat is well-marbled or not. Choose those cuts of meat that are red and not pink in colour.

Besides, if you follow the blood group diet, you must already know that lean beef is actually good for those who belong to the O blood group. So there is more than one way of looking at red meat after all!

Lean beef fillet 500 g (1 lb 1½ oz)

Light soy sauce 1 tsp

Rice wine 1 Tbsp

Chinese (Napa) cabbage half a head

DIPPING SAUCE (COMBINE INGREDIENTS)

Light soy sauce 4 Tbsp

Juice from half a lemon

Red chilli 1, sliced thinly

Fresh coriander (cilantro) 1 sprig, coarsely chopped

Spring onion (scallion) 1, sliced thinly

1. Place beef in the freezer for a little while to harden it up and make it easier to slice. Slice meat as thinly as you can.

2. Season with light soy sauce and rice wine. Refrigerate and leave to marinate covered overnight, or for a few hours.

3. Wash cabbage and cut off the hard stems, keeping for another use. Cut leaves and tender stems into small pieces. Bring a kettle of water to the boil and blanch cabbage leaves.

4. Bring a wok half-filled with water to boil. Meanwhile, lay beef slices evenly onto the rack of a small or medium-sized Chinese bamboo steaming basket. Top with a layer of cabbage leaves.

5. When water boils, place basket, covered, on a plate and place it on a rack in the wok. Cover wok and leave to steam for 10 minutes, or less if you prefer rare beef. While food is being steamed, prepare dipping sauce by combining ingredients together.

6. Remove from heat and serve immediately with lemon-flavoured soy sauce dip with spring onion, red chilli and fresh coriander.

serves 8

fish and
seafood

for many of us, a simple fried fish
is everyday food, yet few know that
it adds more than protein to a diet.
fish is a recommended food in a heart
healthy diet, delivering valuable omega-3
fats to the diner. the recommendation is
to eat oily fish—sardines, mackerel,
tuna and mullet—at least twice a week.
even munching on edible fish bones has
a benefit—sardine bones, for example,
has lots of calcium and vitamin d.

smoked cod in a parcel

Some people just do not like fish except perhaps when it is deep-fried. Fish, however, can also be smoked. Here fresh cod is tea-smoked, giving an unusual musky, smoky flavour to the fish, which is seasoned with just salt and pepper. Yet it is not bland at all, thanks to the inherent rich flavour of cod.

Now do not throw up your hands in horror at the thought of smoking a fish. It is simpler than you think. And it gives us one more cooking option for fish, aside from frying, steaming, boiling, baking and grilling, that is. Home smoking, which used to be a way to preserve foods, offers a different and delicious flavour to fish, if it is lightly done, which it is, in this case.

While any medium can be used for smoking, (some restaurants use rice stalks and husks, for example) I like Chinese tea leaves because it is easily on hand and gives me another way to use up my tea leaves that seems to last forever in the larder! All you need is a covered wok and some aluminium foil to protect the wok. Basically, you have to heat the tea leaves until it smokes. Wetting the dried tea leaves helps, just like wet leaves on a bonfire.

Since everything is done on gentle heat, you will need to bake it to cook it completely. Of course if you choose sashimi quality fish, you could eat it there and then, but baking the smoked fish with mushrooms adds another dimension to the taste.

Besides, it is truly a olfactory delight to open the packet and get that whiff of aromatic smoke. While some people believe that there is a link between smoked foods and cancer, this fish is so lightly smoked that few carcinogens would have built up in the smoke. As always, moderation is the key; besides, there is a definite benefit from eating fish.

People who eat fish at least twice a week, if not more, have a much lower risk of heart disease and heart attack than people who don't eat fish. Cod, specifically, promotes cardiovascular health because it is a good source of healthy omega-3 fatty acids. These healthy fats, which are found in oily fish, can do wonderful things such as lower blood pressure, triglycerides (fat in the blood), and preventing blood clots. Plus it contributes towards reducing inflammation and joint pain. What's there not to like about fish really?

Chinese black tea leaves ½ cup

Sugar 1 Tbsp

Fresh cod fillet 100 g (3½ oz), deboned

Salt for seasoning

Crushed black pepper for seasoning

Abalone mushrooms 2, caps and stems wiped with a damp paper towel

Coriander (cilantro) leaves to garnish

Greaseproof paper two A4-sized sheets

1. Preheat oven to 160°C (325°F).

2. Moisten tea leaves with water. Dust with sugar and mix well. Place moistened tea leaves in a wok lined with aluminium foil. Place a perforated steamer plate within. Cover wok and gently heat until tea leaves begin to smoke.

3. Meanwhile, cut cod fillet into two pieces and rub in salt and pepper to taste. When tea leaves start to smoke, place seasoned fish directly on the steamer plate. Turn off heat, replace wok cover and smoke fish for 10 minutes.

4. Remove cod and place on sheet of greaseproof paper. Top with mushrooms, seasoned with a pinch of salt and pepper each. Fold paper over fish and mushrooms to make a parcel.

5. Place parcel with loose ends tucked under in oven and bake for five minutes.

6. If serving more people, repeat the above steps, multiplying the fish pieces and the parcels.

7. Serve wrapped parcel, as is, allowing your guest to unwrap it and enjoy that aromatic whiff of smoked fish. Offer chopped fresh coriander leaves as a garnish.

serves 1-2

salmon confit in lemon and ginger oil

I am not fond of salmon, but I will eat this fish. Cooked gently in oil until its texture changes but still remains silky and soft, it is a triumph of taste and textures.

The dish takes just 15 minutes, despite its rather sophisticated presentation. You could rely on more complicated seasonings, but here I have reduced the flavours to just two—lemon and ginger—while the accompanying zucchini salad takes off from a Japanese classic of vinegared cucumber and wakame seaweed. I chose zucchini over cucumber because it is less watery.

Tasty and healthy dishes that are also easy to produce are hard to find, so I was thrilled to include this one in my repertoire.

It cannot help but be tasty—you take a slab of fresh salmon (or better still, ocean trout), infuse the best olive oil you can find with ginger and lemon, and use it to poach the fish in oven on low heat.

Thanks to the gentle cooking, the flavour of the fish is retained, the texture turns silky while the flavoured oil adds oomph. The vinegared zucchini and wakame salad gives piquant contrast.

And really what could be more healthful than fresh fish, simply cooked? From the salmon, you get good fats, the healthful omega-3 fats, protein and also minerals—a serving of salmon contains over half of the necessary B12 vitamin, niacin, and selenium, and is an excellent source of B6 and magnesium.

Not only that, zucchini (or courgettes) supply useful amounts of folic acid and potassium, while kelp, which is what wakame is, contains valuable iodine. The recommendation is to eat it 2–3 times a week.

Despite all this goodness, let me assure you that the dish does not look nor taste like health food at all. You will get cries of appreciation round the table when you bring it out.

Salt ½ tsp

Crushed black pepper to taste

Skinless fresh salmon fillets 4, about 150 g (5⅓ oz)

Lemon rind from 1 lemon

Ginger 30 g (1 oz), peeled and shaved using a potato peeler

Olive oil enough to cover salmon fillets

ZUCCHINI SEAWEED SALAD

Dried wakame seaweed 25 g (¾ oz), reconstituted in water for about 10 minutes

Zucchini 1, cut in strips lengthwise using a potato peeler

Rice vinegar 4 Tbsp

Salt 1 tsp

Sugar 2 tsp

1. Heat the oven to 60°C (140°F) or the lowest temperature on the dial.

2. Rub salt and pepper over salmon and leave aside for at least 30 minutes.

3. Place lemon rind and ginger shavings in an oven-proof casserole dish and pour enough oil to reach halfway of the sides of the dish. Cover dish and warm oil for 5–7 minutes or until it reaches the oven's temperature.

4. Place fish in oil and cover dish. Place in oven and cook for 10 minutes. Remove dish from oven, turn fish over and return to oven to cook in the residual heat. When ready to serve, cut each fillet into two.

5. Meanwhile, prepare zucchini wakame salad. Squeeze out water from the reconstituted wakame and place in a bowl. Add zucchini shavings. Dress with vinegar, salt and sugar. Leave aside for a while for flavours to develop.

6. Mound salad on a plate and top with a piece of poached salmon. Add a swirl of the lemon and ginger oil and serve at once.

serves 8

steamed snapper with lime, garlic and chilli

I love Thai flavours, except that the dishes all have to be eaten with rice. And rice, bread and potatoes are a no-no these days with low-carb being all the rage.

Well, I have worked out a recipe for a Thai steamed fish that is not too overpowering nor over-spicy. Instead it is light and tangy, adjectives that you would not normally associate with Thai food—and green with fresh herbs. It is a fish I could eat on its own, that is, without rice. While the Thais have several fish recipes, many of them are deep-fried, hardly an everyday option, aside from the oily mess it produces in the kitchen, or come bathed in heavy spicy sauces.

This one is plainly steamed with just garlic, lime and green chilli and served with a generous topping of fresh herbs. That combination alone is enough to make my mouth water. The fish, though steamed with not an iota of oil, is far from bland, while the handfuls of fresh herbs, which I throw in gives it an uplifting finish. While you could use a sea bass or even the rich cod for this recipe, I use a pink snapper, a fish with sweet but light tasting flesh. It is not too rich to eat on its own; in other words, perfect food for a low-carb dieter.

Steaming fish requires precision timing—just 8 minutes for a medium-sized fish and no more. You want flesh that is slightly pink at the bone. For those who worry about undercooking it, remember that the fish continues to cook in the residual heat even after you have removed it from the wok.

While you need to place slices of lime, garlic and chilli in the stomach cavity of the fish to allow its flavours to penetrate the flesh, do hold some back to garnish later. You want their fresh colours to jazz up the presentation, though I must say that the fresh coriander, mint and basil, added at the last minute, did wonders as well for the look.

Whole pink snapper 1, about 1 kg (2 lb 3 oz), cleaned

Garlic 2 cloves, peeled and sliced

Large green limes 4 (2 sliced thinly)

Green chillies 4, chopped

Fish sauce 2 Tbsp

Sugar 1 tsp

Water or chicken stock 250 ml (8 fl oz / 1 cup)

Fresh mint, coriander (cilantro) and Thai sweet basil leaves 1 small bunch each

1. Wash snapper thoroughly and make two horizontal slashes in the body. Rub a pinch of salt and pepper all over and in the belly cavity.

2. Stuff the belly cavity with half of garlic slices, lime slices and chopped green chillies. Leave the rest aside for garnish later.

3. Bring a wok half-filled with water to the boil.

4. Meanwhile, roll the remaining 2 limes on a clean work surface, pressing down to release the juices inside. Cut into half and squeeze juice into a cup. Add fish sauce, sugar and water or stock.

5. Pluck leaves only from mint and coriander bunches. Tear basil leaves into small pieces. Put herbs aside. They should fill about two cups.

6. When water in the wok is boiling, place fish in a deep dish that can fit into the wok. Pour fish sauce mixture over and steam, covered, for 8 minutes. Remove from heat and serve immediately, garnished lavishly with fresh herbs and the rest of the garlic, chilli and lime slices.

7. Served this way, this steamed fish is pretty and tasty with not an iota of extra oil added. Just offer a lightly dressed salad or sautéed greens on the side to make a complete meal. And no rice!

serves 2-4

fish quenelles

There is a *yong tau fu* stall in Chinatown selling stuffed bean curd that is quite different.

Still stuffed with fish, the filling is soft and yielding, unlike the bouncy textures that we're used to. Our fish products have this crunchiness, which some foreigners find really strange as it feels like biting into a rubber ball!

However, there is this French fish cake that is soft and smooth like a fish mousse. I have never forgotten my first taste of quenelles, as these fish cakes are called, more than 10 years ago.

Quenelles are usually made with cream, hence their creaminess, and so are not advised if you are lactose intolerant or are on a low-fat diet. Omit it, however, and they are perfect food for a health-conscious person, as they are made of fish mostly, and are poached to a silky softness.

Furthermore, homemade quenelles are not loaded with flavour enhancers, which unfortunately a lot of our fish products are. Neither is there added flour, another practice I loathe in commercial fish cakes, as I try to be wheat-free as much as possible.

So when snapper fillets were on offer recently, I decided to attempt my own recipe for quenelles. I omitted the cream and relied on just wine and finely chopped shallots for flavour. I used the food chopper to blend the mixture, though some care is needed here, for too much processing would result in that crunchiness that I am trying to avoid.

The poaching liquid is also important. You could use water, but stock, seafood or vegetable, gives better flavour. The liquid must stay at a simmering level throughout for that barely there consistency.

You could eat the quenelles on their own, but they are delicious dressed with a green coriander and spring onion oil.

Shallots 2, peeled

Boneless snapper fillet 200 g (7 oz), sliced

Egg 1

Light olive oil 1 tsp

Cold water 1 Tbsp

Rice wine 1 Tbsp

Salt a pinch

Ground white pepper ½ tsp

Water, fish or vegetable stock about 4 cups

White wine 4 Tbsp

Coriander (cilantro) leaves 2 sprigs

Spring onion (scallions) 2

Young ginger 2 slices

Extra virgin olive oil 250 ml (8 fl oz / 1 cup)

Sea salt 1 tsp

Ground black pepper to taste

Pickled capers (optional) 1 Tbsp

1. Chop shallots and fish in a food processor. When smooth, add egg and process again. Add oil, cold water (for a softer finish) and rice wine. Process for a few bursts until paste is smooth. Do not overdo this step as fish paste would otherwise become rubbery.

2. Transfer mixture to a bowl and season with salt and pepper. If a smoother texture is desired, strain mixture through a sieve.

3. In a pot, bring water or stock to boil. Add quarter cup of white wine. When water boils, reduce heat. Scoop up a mound of fish paste using a tablespoon and using another spoon, smoothen the top. Using the spoons, slip egg-shaped fish paste into the simmering water or stock. Repeat, cooking in two batches until paste is used up. Quenelles are cooked when they float to the surface.

4. Carefully remove quenelles, drain on kitchen paper and place on a plate. Chill until ready to serve. Meanwhile, place coriander sprigs, spring onions and ginger in a processor. Add olive oil, sea salt and pepper and process until a green oil forms.

5. Serve quenelles on a plate. Top with coriander oil. Garnish with pickled capers for a shot of sharpness.

serves 4-5

nyonya bouillabaisse

Seafood is good for us in so many ways, but the problem is that we lack imagination cooking it. Inevitably, we fry or steam it. Very few of us braise, poach or boil it for fear of it turning out too 'fishy'.

Thai tom yum soup is essentially a boiled fish soup with herbs, while the Peranakans have recipes where the seafood is cooked in a spiced stock. The French also have bouillabaisse, a hearty fish stew where all manner of seafood is cooked in a tomato broth, redolent with herbs and olive oil. The common ingredient for these is the use of spices and herbs, which means that any 'fishiness', a common worry, is masked. Of course, if you are adept at choosing seafood, there is no worry about fishy smells.

There is no big secret about finding fresh fish. Generally if the eyes look bright and the flesh feels firm and shiny, it is fresh. In other words, it must look like a thing of beauty. When it is fish day in our household, I will visit the market that morning to pick up a fish, maybe some shellfish or prawns to cook that night.

Instead of frying or steaming, I may cook them in a pot together with vegetables making it an easy one-dish meal. To ring in the changes, I may make a fish stew with local flavours.

Here I marry two traditions by spicing up a Mediterranean broth with a sambal, which I will either make from scratch or put together with the help of a bottled paste. Whichever, I will end up with a full-bodied stew. If you are worried about cholesterol, add more fish and less of the rest. Besides, the final choice really depends on what is available in the market that day.

Clams or mussels 12

Large squid 1 cut into rings

Spanish mackerel (*ikan batang*) 2 steaks, cut into at least 6 pieces

Prawns 12, peeled, shells reserved for making seafood stock

Red capsicum (bell pepper) 1

Green capsicum (bell pepper) 1

Green zucchini 1

Baby corn 12

Tomatoes 4, chopped

Brown onion 1, peeled and chopped

Tamarind purée 1 Tbsp

Water or seafood stock (made from boiling prawn shells with the water) 6 cups

Salt 1 tsp

Sugar 1 tsp

Ground black or white pepper to taste

SPICE PASTE

Shallots 1 cup, peeled

Red chillies 2–3

Dried prawn (shrimp) paste (*belacan*) 1 Tbsp

Turmeric powder 1 tsp

Galangal powder 1 Tbsp

serves 6

1. Soak clams or mussels in a basin of water for 30 minutes or so to allow any grit to flow out.

2. Clean squid and cut into rings. Cut fish into 6 pieces. Remove clams or mussels from soaking water and scrub clean under running water. If using mussels, pull off the beards.

3. Store prepared seafood, covered in the fridge until needed.

4. Prepare vegetables. Cut capsicums into half and remove the seeds and white membrane within. Cut into bite-sized pieces. Cut zucchini into matching pieces and trim off the hard ends of the baby corn.

5. Prepare spice paste. Place peeled shallots, chilli and dried prawn paste in a food processor and process until fine. Mix in turmeric and galangal powders. Set aside.

6. Heat 1 Tbsp olive oil in a pot large enough for the seafood. Fry spice paste over low heat until fragrant. Add tomato and onion and cook until softened.

7. Add tamarind, water or stock. Bring mixture to the boil and put in clams or mussels. Cover pot for a few minutes until their shells open. Discard any unopened shells.

8. Add vegetables and return stock to the boil before adding the rest of the seafood. Season with salt, sugar and pepper and remove from heat. The ingredients will cook nicely in the residual heat.

9. Serve with rice or crusty bread to dunk into this spicy stew and you will never complain about seafood being boring again.

hot and sour sri lankan fish soup

An English friend once cried out petulantly to me: "What's the matter with you Singaporeans, you put chilli into everything!" She was right. We love chilli and the spicier the better. Stories abound of Singaporeans who pack chilli flakes when travelling to cooler climes and others who will ask for chilli even when eating Western food.

My brother even has a tip for losing weight: just forgo chilli in the food. It is pathetic but true. Leave out the chilli and the appetite suddenly diminishes.

The reasons for this preference are rooted in our beginnings. In Asian countries, where rice is a staple and budgets small, spice helps stretch the food. All we need is a bit of curried gravy or sambal with rice to fill our stomachs. Add sourness to the dish and the appetite quotient rises even more. Another friend will order tom yum soup at every meal when visiting Thailand, so beloved is he of the spicy and sour soup. I have news for him and others of his ilk: the Sri Lankans have a similar soup, made with fish, but it is no bland offering.

This soup is addictive, for it is hot with chillies and black pepper, sour with a tamarind-like fruit called kokum, and rich with fish flavours. Plus it is easy to turn out, taking just five minutes from start to finish. It certainly can be the highlight of any Singaporean meal, so pleasing are the tastes to our palates.

While any fish can be used, the less common golden or silver pomfret is recommended as it is a full-flavoured fish, full of healthy omega-3 and 6 fats. While the Sri Lankans use kokum, a black dried fruit, akin to mangosteen skin, to add sourness to the pot, we can use tamarind which is more easily available. Kokum, a condiment native to coastal South India and Sri Lanka, can however be bought in Little India. Importantly, do make sure the chilli powder that is the mainstay of this soup is fiery hot. You should obtain Sri Lankan chilli powder, which uses a hotter variety of chilli, or else check with the stallholder on the spice levels. It turns this fish soup into a full-frontal assault on the tastebuds!

Golden pomfret 1, medium-sized

Salt 1 tsp

Hot chilli powder 1 Tbsp

Ground black pepper 1 tsp

Curry leaves 2 sprigs

Screwpine (*pandan*) leaf 1 cut into pieces

Water 1–1.25 litres (40–48 fl oz / 4–5 cups), or enough to just cover the fish

Kokum 4–5 pieces, soaked in a little water over a few days to rehydrate, or use 1 Tbsp bottled tamarind purée

Tomatoes 4–5, cut into quarters

1. Clean fish and make two slashes on the body. Rub about 1 tsp salt all over. Set aside.

2. Place chilli powder, pepper, curry leaves and screwpine leaves in a pot. Add water and redydrated kokum fruit or tamarind purée. Bring to the boil and cook for a few minutes until the spices meld together. Season with a little salt to taste.

3. Add fish and tomatoes and turn off the heat. After a few minutes, add a fresh sprig of curry leaves to garnish if desired. Serve with rice.

serves 4-5

cha ca la vong

For those who do not know, this is a world-famous fish dish, listed under as one of the 1,000 things you have to do before you die, in a book of the same name by travel writer Patricia Schultz. It is the quintessential Hanoi dish—fish, dill, spring onions and turmeric, fried in a small pan atop a charcoal brazier. But the combination of spiced fish, fresh herbs and cold noodles tossed in hot aromatic oil is unbeatable. And it can be healthy eating if you do not overdo the oil and increase the greens quotient.

I first ate it 10 years ago in the original restaurant in the Old Quarter on Cha Ca Street, which was named after the dish. These days you can find a branch in Ho Chi Minh City and elsewhere within Hanoi itself, but the original at No. 14 is quite an eating experience. The dish originated over 100 years ago in the Doan family restaurant in Hanoi. You walk up a flight of rickety stairs and enter a rather dilapidated and ancient dining room where only one dish is on offer.

This is the fish—traditionally, catfish presented in a hot pan filled with sizzling oil. The waiter proceeds to soften handfuls of fresh dill and spring onion in the pan. To eat, you take a little of the sauteed fish and fresh herbs, put it over cold rice vermicelli (bun), add more fresh herbs, mainly dill, coriander and mint, and toss it all.

Despite the fame of the dish, it is actually quite easy to turn out. I just sauté rather than deep-fry the fish slices—I chose snakehead, now easily available in the market—seasoned first with turmeric and galangal powder, then fresh spring onions and dill are added. I also offer more fresh greens than the original.

All this can be done over the stove. The frypan can then taken out to the table, together with the cold noodles and the greens, for guests to help themselves to. The rice noodles should be Vietnamese, but the thick laksa *bee hoon* is an acceptable substitute, though it is more al dente.

The health benefits of eating fish are well known, as well as the benefits of eating raw greens. Just hold back on the oil and the simple carbohydrate, which *bee hoon* is, and this world famous fish can come home to you.

Thick-cut fish steaks such as *ikan batang* or snakehead (*toman*) fish 500 g (1 lb 1½ oz)

Turmeric powder 1 tsp

Galangal powder 1 Tbsp

Fish sauce 1 Tbsp

Rice wine 1 Tbsp

Dried Vietnamese rice noodles (or substitute with thick laksa *bee hoon*), 400 g (14⅓ oz), boiled

Vegetable oil ½ cup

Fresh dill 100 g (3½ oz), chopped roughly

Spring onions (scallions) 1 bunch, sliced into 4-cm (2-in) lengths

Butter lettuce leaves 1 head

Mixed herbs (fresh dill, basil, mint and coriander [cilantro] leaves) a generous amount

Red chillies 5–6, sliced

DIPPING SAUCE (COMBINE INGREDIENTS)

Prawn (shrimp) purée (*har cheong* paste) 4–6 Tbsp

Sugar 1–2 tsp

Lime juice to taste

1. Cut fish steaks into thick slices and rub with turmeric and galangal powders. Season with fish sauce and rice wine. Leave for at least an hour. Bring a pot of water to boil. When boiling, place the dried rice noodles within and cook until it softens.

2. Drain, then dunk noodles in cold water to arrest the cooking process and to allow the starch to be washed out. Drain again and leave aside. Heat vegetable oil in a frying pan and when hot, quickly sauté the fish. When fish changes colour, add fresh dill and spring onions. Allow to wilt and bring the whole pan out to the table.

3. To serve: each person takes a portion of noodles and tops it with fish slices, wilted herbs and some oil. Noodles are garnished with a selection of butter lettuce leaves, mixed herbs and cut chilli.

4. Add a teaspoonful of dipping sauce to the mixture. Toss and enjoy.

serves 4–6

cured salmon with garlic and chilli

There's something utterly decadent about eating in bed and the festive season is a time when we partake of a festive brunch—champagne (or sparkling wine, at least) and cured salmon usually—while watching a frothy holiday movie in bed!

Despite this dip into festive frivolity, there is actually no need to exercise restraint in eating—Christmassy foods are inherently healthy, with turkey (the most low-fat meat you can find, we are now told) and yes, salmon on the menu.

I cure my own salmon—that is, I preserve it by cooking it in a bit of salt and sugar. Now that fresh salmon is easily available and quite affordable, I find it cheaper, tastier and even healthier to make my own. And it is easy. The fishmonger will fillet and remove all the pin bones from the fish and it takes just 5 minutes to rub salt and sugar into the flesh, before storing it in the refrigerator for a couple of days.

The cured fish can be eaten on its own, or with a sweetened mustard (just add sugar to the commercial variety, thinned down with vinegar or water) or a salad dressing of your choice. You can also add garnishes—traditional toppings are capers, chopped egg and some thinly sliced onions. I prefer to eat it with just a drizzle of chopped garlic and chilli (deseeded) oil. The taste then takes off.

Salmon used to be a luxury food, especially when only the wild variety was sold. Nowadays with farmed fish, the costs have been brought down and you can eat it even everyday! It is of course the ideal health food, being an excellent source of omega-3 fatty acids, vitamin D, and selenium. It is also has protein, niacin and vitamin B12 and high levels of phosphorous, magnesium and vitamin B6.

Just be sure to buy absolutely fresh fish. I usually get a fish from the freezer, then ask for a fillet or even a whole side, if I am going to feed a lot of people. The amount of salt used for the curing is usually 5 per cent of the weight of the fish, so if it is a 500 g (1 lb 1½ oz) fish, you need just 25 g (¾ oz) of sea salt or about 1½ Tbsp. I like to add an equal amount of sugar to the cure to give a softer finish. Top it with whichever garnishes or dressing you prefer and serve. In bed, of course!

Fresh salmon loin 250 g (9 oz) skin left intact

Rock sea salt just under 1 Tbsp

Sugar 1 Tbsp

GARLIC AND CHILLI OIL

Garlic 1 clove

Red chilli 1, deseeded

Light olive oil 2 Tbsp

GARNISH

Mesclun lettuce or mixed salad leaves 1 cup

Simple vinaigrette dressing (a combination of olive oil, salt, pepper and lemon juice to taste) 1 Tbsp

Coriander (cilantro) leaves 2 sprigs

Lemon (optional) ½, cut into small wedges

1. Dry salmon with paper towels and place, skin down, on a plate.

2. Rub salt and sugar into the flesh. Wrap fish in plastic wrap and place on a plate with two unopened cans of beans or similar item on top to weigh it down.

3. Leave fish in the fridge at least overnight and up to three days.

4. On the day of serving, scrape off the salt and sugar dressing. The fish will exude some moisture, so dry it with paper towels again. Remove the skin and slice flesh thinly across the grain.

5. Lay fish slices on a plate. Make your garlic chilli oil by chopping garlic and deseeded chilli together and adding the oil. Allow to infuse for about 10 minutes. Pour it over the sliced fish, just before serving.

6. Garnish with mesclun lettuce or mixed salad leaves, dressed with vinaigrette dressing, topped with fresh coriander leaves and with lemon wedges on the side, if liked.

serves 6

binjai geram assam

The durian takes so much of the spotlight when it is in season that few realise the month also heralds the season of the *binjai*. This is an old-fashioned and now forgotten fruit, equally pungent in its aroma. And people who know would be waiting for it to fall in the wooded areas of, where else, Binjai Park, that housing estate so named after the many *binjai* trees in the area. Also known as the Malaysian mango (*mangifera caesia*), the *binjai*, its Malay name, is a species of mango found not only in Singapore, but also in Malaysia, Brunei, Papua New Guinea and the Philippines. But what concerns us here is how it can make fish appetising even to non-fish eaters.

I have written about how one can make a fresh sambal from the fruit, to be eaten with fried fish (see page 91). Less well-known is the practice of lightly cooking the fruit, together with a fish, in a spicy tamarind gravy. The gravy is actually the Peranakan classic called *geram assam*, a dish so delectable that it is irresistible, which is what its Malay name means.

The spice paste is lightly fried to caramelise the spices, before tamarind is added, but here, *binjai* is added to give that sweet, sour and strangely rich tang, melting eventually into the gravy. And if you're lucky enough to get a ripe fruit, (choose the longish fruit which is sweeter) the gravy turns ambrosial. You need not go into the undergrowth around Binjai Park to get your pickings. The markets at Joo Chiat and Tekka would sell this native mango, which is characterised by its speckled brown skin and white flesh. Soft to the touch when ripe, it should then be refrigerated. Wrap it well in a plastic bag, however, or else its strong smell will permeate the entire fridge like a durian!

I chose king mackerel (*ikan batang*) for this recipe for two reasons: it is less boney and rich enough to match the strong flavours of the fruit, but you could use a whole fish such as pomfret or a snapper instead. The use of a fruit to sweeten and in this case, enrich a gravy lessens the need for sugar and creates a full mouthful without relying on the usual agents of cream or coconut milk. And we are not even taking into account yet, of the fruit's nutritional advantages. It adds fibre, antioxidants and vitamin C to the pot, all good things for a healthful diet indeed. And for these, there is always a season!

Salt 1 tsp

King mackerel (*ikan batang*) 600 g (1 lb 5⅓ oz) cut into 6 steaks

***Binjai* fruit** 2

Lemon grass 1 stalk, ends trimmed, hard outer leaves removed and smashed

Water 1 litre (32 fl oz / 4 cups)

Salt 1 tsp or to taste

Tamarind purée 1 Tbsp or to taste

Sugar 1 tsp or to taste

SPICE PASTE

Shallots 1 cup, peeled

Red chillies 2–3

Dried prawn (shrimp) paste (*belacan*) 1 Tbsp

Turmeric powder 1 tsp

Galangal powder 1 Tbsp

1. Rub salt over fish. Peel *binjai* fruit and cut out large slices of the flesh, discarding the seed. Leave both aside.

2. Prepare spice paste. Process ingredients in a food processor until fine. Heat 1 Tbsp vegetable oil in a pot and fry spice paste over low heat until fragrant and oil begins to exude.

3. Add lemon grass stalk. After a few minutes, add water and increase heat. When gravy comes to the boil, add the fish, then the *binjai* slices. Add salt, then taste.

4. Depending on the ripeness of the fruit, you may need to add the tamarind purée and the sugar. Otherwise, leave well alone and serve hot with rice and some *sambal belachan*, that chilli and toasted prawn paste condiment.

serves 6-8

binjai salsa

Buah binjai can be made into a fresh sambal that is traditionally served with a fried fish. And these fresh or uncooked sambals have many healthful characteristics. As they are uncooked, the nutrients of the fruit are retained, resulting in an unadulterated delivery of vitamin C and other antioxidants.

Here I have updated the traditional recipe as the original calls for copious amounts of black soy sauce, creating a rather murky concoction.

Taking my inspiration from guacamole, I add shallots and green chilli to the mashed *binjai* which make for a visual as well as a gustatory delight.

This fresh sambal is then served with fried fish, an old-fashioned idea that is most welcome even today.

Binjai fruit 1

Shallots 2, peeled and sliced thinly

Green chillies 2, sliced

Salt ½ tsp

Sugar 1 tsp or more, depending on the ripeness of the fruit

1. Peel and cut slices off *binjai* fruit. It will not shred, but is quite easily mashed.

2. Place fruit in a bowl. Top with shallots and green chillies. Season with salt and sugar. Mash everything together and taste to adjust seasoning if needed. Serve with a plain fried fish or as an appetiser with crackers or tortilla chips.

makes 1 cup

spicy fish wantons

We have meat dumplings, vegetarian dumplings and prawn dumplings but why are there no fish dumplings? And yet fish cake and fish balls, both made from fish, are readily available, though I worry about the amounts of monosodium glutamate (MSG) found in these products. But enticed by the special offer of snapper fillets at the supermarket recently, I bought a few pieces and attempted a recipe for fish wantons. Already we like fish and we like it any way—fried, steamed, boiled or poached. Now I discover we like it also wrapped in a wanton skin.

There are many advantages of wrapped food—protected from direct heat, it retains its juiciness and sweetness. The flour skin gives a nice foil to the flavour and adds body to the bite. While the palate, especially of non-fish eaters, can be bored by eating just fish, fry it in some batter or wrap it with an edible wrapper and suddenly it becomes appetising. While the seasoning for the fish meat is Chinese, the dressing is not. It is a Southeast Asian chilli oil, redolent with the scent of prawn paste and onion. Living in the tropics, our taste buds have been irrevocably changed by our neighbours and we cannot eat a dish without some bite on the side.

While fish is, of course, widely touted to be good for the health—it is high in protein, low in saturated fats and contains healthy omega-3 essential acids which protect against heart disease, cancer and Alzheimer's disease—so is chilli. The capsaicin in chilli—that is the white ribs of a chilli, protects us from cancer and is rich with vitamin C, which is an antioxidant. So that taste for chilli, picked up from the spice eaters in our midst, is a blessing and certainly helps these less-than-common fish wantons to go down easily.

FILLING

Shallots 2, peeled
Boneless snapper fillet 200 g (7 oz), sliced
Egg 1
Sesame oil 1 tsp
Cold water 1 Tbsp
Rice wine 1 Tbsp
Salt a pinch
White pepper to taste
Bamboo shoots (optional) ½ cup, chopped finely
Water for boiling wantons
Round wheat dumpling wrappers 24

CHILLI DRESSING (COMBINE INGREDIENTS)

Bottled Nyonya sambal chilli 1 Tbsp
Stock (made from boiling wantons in water) ½ cup
Olive oil 1 tsp
Chinese black vinegar 1 tsp

1. Chop peeled shallots in a food processor. When smooth, add half the fish slices. Break a whole egg in and process some more.

2. Add remaining fish, sesame oil, cold water and rice wine. Pulse mixture in a food processor until paste is smooth. Do not overdo this step as the fish texture would otherwise become rubbery. Remove paste and season with salt and pepper. Mix in bamboo shoots if desired.

3. Spray some oil on a flat plate to hold the wrapped wantons. Bring a pot of water or stock to the boil. Meanwhile, fashion wantons by placing a teaspoonful of filling onto the middle of a wrapper. Wet edges and fold over and press to secure edges. Pinch the edges at intervals to get a lacy effect. Place wantons on the oiled plate. When water comes to the boil, add half the dumplings and allow to boil gently till they float up to the surface. Reserve ½ cup stock made from boiling wantons. Remove dumplings and place on a serving plate. Sprinkle some oil over to prevent sticking.

4. Toss dumplings with chilli dressing. Garnish with some chopped coriander and watch this fish product go down in a jiffy!

makes 24

rice and noodles

rice
noodles

carbohydrates is a dirty word these days; but few realise that they are energy-giving, and are fibre-rich foods that are a good source of vitamin b, folate, riboflavin, niacin and thiamin.

the choice of the right carbohydrate to consume is important. generally whole grains have more nutrition than refined grains and the lower the glycemic index of a carbohydrate, the less effect it will have on blood sugar levels.

so if you like your carbs, have them—in moderation, while choosing them wisely!

noodles

steamed custard vermicelli soup

Can Chinese restaurant food be healthy?

Surprisingly, yes. Several of them offer delicious yet healthy options. The entire fish section in the menu is, of course, high in the health stakes, provided they are not deep-fried, as is the vegetables section.

Not only that, there is a plethora of dishes that employ low-fat cooking methods. Not only will you find foods being steamed, but also poached, braised (though these sometimes involve rather large quantities of fat) and increasingly, just dressed with flavoursome vegetable oils. And these dishes are not some sad offering reclining in a corner to be trotted out whenever somebody asks for something light and healthy. No, they are attractions in their own right. I am referring, for example, to that newest craze in high-end restaurants. It is seafood steamed over *mee sua* (fine wheat vermicelli) in a light custard. You get individual serves and the seafood sitting on top could be crayfish, crab or prawn or even an exotic mantis prawn.

What people do not know is that it is also easy to replicate at home. The restaurants use cholesterol-rich crustaceans to top their custards, but here, I use fish, a cream snapper belly. It comes filleted and is rich in flavour. In this, you may like to know that some nutritionists do not believe that the cholesterol in seafood is harmful as it is low-fat food. They believe that it is not cholesterol but rather saturated fats in food that lead to high fat readings in the body, which is why coconut milk is discouraged. It has no cholesterol, but it does have saturated fat, making it the villain of the piece. No matter, the fish is delicious cooked this way.

Steaming is the method of cooking used in this seafood custard soup. An underused mode, it delivers food that is cooked without any addition of oil and yet retains all its sweetness. Here egg white is used to make the light custard below the seafood, rather like a chawan mushi, the Japanese version of egg custard soup. With steaming, timing is critical and yes, a gentle fire. You need just 15 minutes of cooking to set the custard. Don't worry if it seems still watery after that; it will continue to cook in the residual heat and be set beautifully by the time you serve it.

Dried fine wheat vermicelli (*mee sua*) half a skein

Egg whites 2

Homemade or canned chicken stock 250 ml (8 fl oz / 1 cup)

Rice wine 1 Tbsp

Salt a pinch

Sugar a pinch

Cream snapper fillet 20 g (¾ oz)

GARNISHES

Shredded ginger 2.5-cm (1-in) knob, fried until crisp

Dried wolfberries 1 tsp, reconstituted in water and drained

1. Fill a wok with water until it reaches a third of its sides, and bring to the boil. Keep water simmering.

2. In the meantime, bring another small pot of water to boil. When boiling, add *mee sua* and cook until softened. Remove and cool under a running water to arrest its cooking. Divide into two portions. Set aside.

3. Make a custard. Place egg white, chicken stock and rice wine in a small bowl. Season with a pinch of salt (or more if you are using unsalted stock) and sugar. Stir, but do not beat, to combine. Taste and adjust seasoning if needed. This is sufficient for one serve.

4. Rub a pinch of salt over fish. Set aside.

5. Choose a pretty heatproof shallow bowl. Place both portions of *mee sua* in the bowl, top with fish and pour in enough custard to cover noodles.

6. Steam covered in the wok over a medium fire, then turn down to low, when the steaming water starts to boil again. It takes 15 minutes in all.

7. Remove, top with crisp ginger shreds and softened wolfberries and serve immediately.

serves 1

green tea rice

It is not only the Japanese who add green tea to their food. The Taiwanese do it as well. But while the Japanese ladle brewed green tea over rice to make a refreshing rice broth, the Taiwanese sprinkle powdered green tea over fried rice. It delivers an aromatic twist to the dish. The Hakkas, too, make a ground rice tea soup called *lei cha fan*. This is essentially a green tea soup to which herbs, ground nuts, rice and soy beans are added. The Burmese, however, have a pickled tea called *lepet* (you can buy these fermented tea leaves in a jar). A dollop of this moreish tea leaf paste is served on top of chopped or sliced tomato, garnished with a host of delicious crunchies such as fried shallots and garlic, nuts and dried prawns. It is an energising dish because there is caffeine in green tea even if you eat rather than drink it, something people forget.

All these methods of using green tea give us more ways to consume this antioxidant, aside from just drinking it, that is. And we cannot have too many. Green tea is now known to be a powerful antioxidant, better than grape juice or red wine. Less processed than black tea, its phytochemicals contain rich antioxidants that protect the body's cells from damage and fight disease. They are said to prevent cancer, reduce the risk of strokes, heart disease and even help to lower blood cholesterol.

If green tea is now your beverage of choice as it is with me, do steep the tea bag for at least three minutes to allow the antioxidants to seep into the liquid. And if you're concerned about caffeine, a cup of green tea contains just 30 mg as compared to coffee's 100 mg per cup.

Following the Taiwanese, my green tea rice also relies on green tea, but instead of powdered tea, I make a paste from soaked tea leaves. It certainly adds more flavour to the dish as the leaves are marinated first in a mixture of oil, salt and, if liked, chilli powder, an addictive combo.

Like a pesto, it is then tossed together with the boiled rice, together with pork or chicken and green bean, making it a balanced one-dish meal. A garnish of roasted peanuts and onions add delicious crunch.

Now you can drink your tea and eat it!

GREEN TEA PASTE

Japanese or Chinese green tea leaves ½ cup

Salt 1 tsp

Vegetable oil ¼ cup

Sesame oil 1 tsp

Lemon ½, squeezed for juice

INGREDIENTS

Vegetable oil 1 tsp

Chopped garlic 1 tsp

Minced chicken 200 g (7 oz)

Long beans 2 cups, chopped

Salt 1 tsp

Cooked Basmati rice 2 cups

GARNISHES

Roasted peanuts

Crisp fried shallots

1. Prepare green tea paste. Pour hot water over tea leaves. Leave for 3 minutes or so till they soften. Drain and squeeze dry (you can keep the tea for drinking).

2. Place drained tea leaves in a food processor and add salt, oils and lemon juice. Process until well blended. Taste and adjust seasoning, if needed. Leave aside for flavours to meld together.

3. Meanwhile, heat 1 oil in a wok and brown garlic. Add chicken, followed by long beans. Season with salt. Toss this with the cooked rice and mix well.

4. To serve, place a dollop of green tea paste on top of the rice. Garnish with nuts and fried shallots. Toss before serving and adjust seasoning to taste.

serves 4

japanese oat porridge

There are oats and oats. If you have been confused, like me, by the array on the shelves, a good principle is to buy oats that are minimally processed. So this rules out your quick cooking oats and even your rolled oats, which have been steamed, then rolled to flatten them.

This makes them easier to cook, but it also robs them of some of the B vitamins. I now buy pinhead oats, also known as steel-cut oats, where the grain is merely cut into smaller bits for easier cooking This retains the crunchiness of the cereal, which I like. While some people resort to soaking the grains overnight to make cooking easier, I find that simmering the oats for 20 minutes is all that it needs.

Both rolled oats and steel cut oats are whole grains, which are healthy for you. Unlike other grains, they contain higher levels of protein, the B vitamins plus calcium, magnesium, iron and zinc. More importantly, they are a good source of soluble fibre and a diet that is low in fat and high in soluble fibre can help reduce blood cholesterol. Oats also have a low glycaemic index that means they are absorbed into the blood stream more slowly, helping to keep blood sugar levels steady.

But truly the best reason for eating them is that they are just delicious and make breaking the fast every morning an adventure.

Rolled or steel-cut oats ¼ cup

Water 250–500 ml (8–16 fl oz / 1–2 cups), depending on preferred consistency of porridge

Salt a pinch

FURIKAKE

Dried salmon flakes (available in packets from Japanese supermarkets) 1 Tbsp

Nori seaweed strips 1 Tbsp

Toasted sesame seeds 1 tsp

Chopped spring onion (scallion) 1 Tbsp

Togarashi seasoning (optional)

1. Place oats in a small pot together with desired amount of water.

2. Bring to the boil, then reduce heat to low, stirring now and then to prevent sticking. Oats should take around 20 minutes to cook.

3. Add salt. Taste to see if you like the consistency. Otherwise cook a little longer.

4. Assemble *furikake* mixture. Combine dried salmon flakes, seaweed strips, sesame seeds and spring onion. Add a shake of *togarashi* seasoning, if you like it spicy. Top oats with mixture.

5. Serve immediately.

Note: Togarashi is a Japanese chilli pepper seasoning.

serves 2

mixed grains mui fan

With the rising price of grains, I am re-looking my menus.

While we are admittedly not great rice eaters, I have been scouring around for a new staple that relies on not just one, but a mixture of grains.

The cancer-fighting macrobiotic diet in fact encourages people to eat more than one kind of grain daily. Over the years, I have been adding barley, millet and wild rice, which is incidentally not rice despite its name, but an aquatic grain that grows wild near rivers and lakes in North America, to rice. And if the yen to eat porridge hits me, it is not white rice porridge that I turn to but oats, which is delicious, especially topped with that Japanese topping called *furikake* (see page 104).

Indeed we do not eat just brown rice, but also rust and black wild rice and barley. It makes for a nutty mouthful and yet is bland enough to form a palette for the other dishes. What is less known is that such mixed grain mixtures can also be made into porridge, fried as in fried rice, made into a pilau, cooked into a risotto or the Chinese version, *mui fan*.

Traditionally, this is boiled rice over which a delicious sauce, made from mixed meats such as pork, prawn and liver or just seafood and vegetable is poured. Here I make a crab and corn sauce for the mixed grains, upping the fibre quotient tremendously. And of course, it cannot help but be delicious, with the sweetness of the corn and crab in the mix.

Mixed grains do take more water and more time to cook, but if you soak them for about 15 minutes first, you hasten the cooking time. While none of this is low-priced foods, they all are very nutritious, which means you get more bang for your buck. Wild rice, for example, is more nutritious than rice containing more than 12 per cent of protein. It also contains more niacin or Vitamin B3 and is a good source of calcium and potassium, and yes, fibre. Equally fibre-rich barley contains vitamin E and more thiamin, riboflavin and lysine than wheat, in this case, making it a more balanced food.

Mixed grains (brown rice, rust and black wild rice) 1 cup

Barley 1 cup

Chicken stock 1 litre, defatted (see article on page 15 for defatting stock)

Corn flour (cornstarch) 1 Tbsp

Rice wine 2 Tbsp

Light soy sauce 1 Tbsp

Salt 1 tsp

Ground white pepper to taste

Chopped corn kernels 1 cup, or use 1 tin creamed corn

Whole corn kernels 1 cup

Pasteurised crabmeat 1 tub

Green peas 1 cup

1. Soak mixed grains and barley in water for about 15 minutes. Drain. Place in a rice cooker and cook with double the amount of water, or 4 cups of water to 2 cups of grains.

2. Bring chicken stock to the boil. Make a paste of the corn flour using a little water and rice wine. Add soy sauce, salt and pepper to taste.

3. Add mixture to the stock, stirring continuously until it thickens. Add chopped corn kernels or creamed corn to the pot.

4. Just before serving, add whole corn kernels, half the crabmeat and green peas.

5. Dish out a small bowl of mixed grains onto a deep plate. Ladle out crab and corn gravy over the rice. If desired, top with extra crabmeat, sliced red chilli and some Chinese parsley. All the *mui fan* flavours you like but over healthier mixed grains!

serves 4-5

spaghetti with tomato, ricotta and pistachios

I went on the much-vaunted Mediterranean diet for the three weeks I was in Sicily recently. And it is as healthy as they say it is. This diet emphasizes fruits and vegetables, nuts, grains, olive oil and grilled chicken and seafood. Plus a glass or two of red wine.

The pasta sauces were a revelation. Since it was Sicily, tomatoes formed the base, but they were not always cooked down into a thick *ragu*. They were also stir-fried or eaten raw in a salad. Truly no worry about my lycopene rations during these weeks! Furthermore I was struck by how the sauces made the most of seasonal ingredients and so one day, we had *pasta alla Norma*, which focuses on the huge Italian eggplants and another day, *pasta le con sarde*, a Palermo classic, which makes the best use of fennel.

Indeed nuts were an important ingredient. While we all know basil pesto, made with almonds, I discovered here a pesto made from pistachios, the best of which incidentally come from Bronte, a town in Sicily. They lend a wonderful nutty fragrance to the plate. I ate a pasta like it on Panarea, a gorgeous island off the Sicilian coast where the beautiful people hang out. Here at a sun-dappled terrace of a restaurant called Da Pina, my friends and I ordered pasta tossed with a tomato sauce and topped with pistachios and salted ricotta. It was unforgettable, for it had never occurred to me before how chopped pistachios could bring new heights to a simple tomato sauce.

Two kinds of tomatoes are used—chopped tomatoes from a can and fresh cherry tomatoes, which are simply halved. The tomatoes are cooked with chopped shrimp, just a few, before being topped with ricotta and a carpet of chopped green pistachios. The pistachios are a brilliant touch for it gives crunch and richness to basically a simple sauce. The salted ricotta, a semi-hard cheese, adds a welcome shot of saltiness.

Yet this is a healthy sauce for it is made mostly from tomatoes and nuts which add protein and also a touch of luxury, a word one does not normally associate with healthy eating. And this is the secret of the Mediterranean diet, good eating that is also inherently healthy.

Dried spaghetti 500 g (1 lb 1½ oz)

Small brown onion 1, peeled and chopped

Garlic 1 clove, peeled and chopped

Prawns 10, peeled, deveined and chopped

Canned chopped tomatoes 1 can, about 400 g (14⅓ oz)

Sugar 1 tsp

Salt 1 tsp

Cherry tomatoes 10, sliced in half

Crumbled ricotta salata 3 Tbsp, or substitute with pecorino cheese

Roasted pistachios 150 g (5⅓ oz), chopped roughly

Crushed black pepper to taste

Mint leaves (optional) for garnish

1. Bring a pot of salted water to boil, then cook spaghetti according to packet instructions. Drain and keep warm.

2. Meanwhile, heat 3 Tbsp extra virgin olive oil in a pan and fry onion and garlic until onions are softened. Add chopped prawns.

3. After a few minutes, add canned tomatoes. Season with salt and sugar. Add cherry tomatoes. Stir well and when softened, turn off heat.

4. Divide drained pasta among 6–8 bowls.

5. Top with tomato sauce, crumble some ricotta or pecorino cheese over, and top with a generous layer of pistachios and black pepper to taste. Serve garnished, if you like, with fresh mint leaves.

serves 6-8

desserts

desserts can be part of a healthy diet and they need not be rich pastries or buttery and creamy cakes. neither do they need to be just fresh fruit, though there is nothing wrong with serving a perfect peach, for example. in my house, i poach or bake fruit or make them into jellies and ices. i also serve dessert soups—full of flavour, no fat and yes, lots of vitamins if you add a fruit to it!

tropical fruit salad with marinated sago pearls

Fruit salads have come a long way. Remember the days when we all ate fruit salad from a tin? While some families still resort to such canned conveniences, fruit salads these days are hopefully healthier—just fresh chopped fruit, sweetened perhaps with light syrup.

Yet while it is healthy, it can also be interesting. The choice of fruit makes a difference. I like to add strawberries and mangoes for a touch of tartness and fragrance. Crunch could come from the hard fruit—apples or pears or even guava. Colour also is important and these days, we have a wide choice of green fruit—kiwis, green apples and grapes or just a scattering of mint leaves—to give a lift to the colour palette. And there are still more ways to add interest to basically just cut fruit.

For a flavoured syrup, I like to infuse the syrup with lemon grass and kaffir lime leaves to give a fresh citrusy flavour. And sometimes, I spike the syrup. My standby during Chinese New Year is a mandarin orange salad, which I marinate lavishly with Cointreau or another orange-flavoured liqueur. Beyond syrups, I like to add unexpected ingredients to the bowl. And so sometimes, I scatter gold raisins or ruby red dried cranberries over the cut fruit. For a bit of creamy tartness, I may scoop out some passion fruit or soursop pulp and drizzle some of that on top.

In this Asian version of a fruit salad, the added interest comes from sago pearls that have been marinated first in delicious palm sugar syrup, spiked with a bit of rum. I wanted the colour and sunlit taste of the tropics in this fruit salad, so I used only papaya and mango. They make a lovely red and orange picture, the colours of sunshine, shot through with some translucent pearls! But this fruit salad is not just a pretty picture. As hinted at by their vibrant colours, the two fruits are chockful of nutrition.

Papaya and mango have no cholesterol nor saturated fat and aside from the carbohydrates, they both contain vitamin A, calcium, iron and fibre that is good for the digestive system and the heart. In addition, they are also rich sources of antioxidant nutrients such as carotenes, vitamin C and flavonoids. Mangoes also contain a wealth of vitamin E and beta-carotene, which promotes the health of the cardiovascular system and also provide protection against colon cancer. And since neither is cooked, all these nutrients are preserved. It makes wonderful advertisement for this tropical fruit salad, aside from taste, that is.

Sago pearls ½ cup

Palm sugar (*gula melaka*), 200 g (7 oz), grated or chopped

Rum 2 Tbsp

Small red papaya 1, peeled, seeds and pith removed and cut into large cubes

Ripe yellow mangoes 4, peeled and cut into large cubes

Mint leaves (optional) for garnish

1. Soak sago for 5 minutes and drain. Bring a small pot of water, enough to cover sago, to the boil. Reduce heat and add sago, stirring continuously until it turn translucent, for about 10 minutes.

2. Drain and rinse pearls under cold running water. Strain and leave aside.

3. Place palm sugar in a pot. Add 375 ml (12 fl oz / 1½ cups) water and bring to the boil. Stir to dissolve sugar, add rum and return to the boil again to burn off the alcohol.

4. When ready to serve, place sago in rum syrup.

5. Place equal amounts of papaya and mango into serving bowls and top with marinated sago pearls. Garnish with mint leaves, if desired.

serves 4

healthy ohr nee

If you can mash potatoes, you can make *ohr nee*, that well-loved Teochew dessert with a long (and to me, undeserved) reputation for being unhealthy. Basically a yam mash sweetened with syrup and then made more interesting with the addition of pumpkin and gingko nuts, it has an appeal that it is more than the sum of these simple ingredients. People love it for its extreme sweetness and its richness, which comes from lard! But few know that you can make that traditional recipe healthier, just by tweaking it a little. While yam or taro remains the bulwark of the sweet offering, I roasted the pumpkin instead of cooking it down to a pulp. I also added rum to the syrup, which traditionally covers the purée, and added it at the last minute so that you can control the amount of sweetness in each helping.

What a blast it turned out to be—all the flavours of *ohr nee* with more style, and certainly more healthy than the traditional version! Admittedly, the mouth feel was lighter, but that was exactly what I was aiming for. Generally after a huge meal, I cannot manage more than a few spoonfuls of *ohr nee* and I want more, much more! For those of you worried about the intake of calories and fat, yam or taro on its own, is low in saturated fat, sodium and cholesterol and is high in all the good things such as dietary fibre, vitamin E, B6, potassium and manganese. As for pumpkin, it is high in antioxidants, particularly beta-carotene—its bright orange colour is a dead giveaway. Not only that, it's also a good source of vitamins C, K and E, and minerals, including magnesium, potassium, and iron.

The first step in making the classic recipe healthier is to omit the lard that traditionally enriches the mash. Those of you reluctant to let go of this step, let me tell you, the updated version is no less flavoursome. Besides who wants to go that extra step of rendering the cubes of pork fat down into oil? Again the old recipes call for shallot oil to be added to the mix. It adds flavour, though the modern-minded among us would find it hard to accept the matching of a savoury onion oil with a sweet. I omitted it but added vanilla instead, which would render its own flavourful oil, more commonly found in desserts.

Finally the recipe is easier to attempt than the old cooks would have you know, or maybe they did not have the modern helps we do? I mean, how hard is it to mash potatoes?

Yam 500 g (1 lb 1½ oz), peeled and cut into large pieces

Salt a pinch

Sugar 2 Tbsp

Light olive oil 100 g (3½ oz)

Pumpkin or butternut squash 500 g (1 lb 1½ oz), peeled and sliced into wedges

SYRUP

Sugar 1 cup

Water 250 ml (8 fl oz / 1 cup)

Peeled gingko nuts 1 cup

Vanilla essence 1 tsp

Rum 1 Tbsp

1. Cut yam into large pieces and place in a pot with enough water to cover. Add salt and sugar, then cook until yam is tender. Drain and reserve boiling water for use later.

2. Mash cooked yam with a fork or in a processor, adding olive oil to round out the taste and some of the boiling water to obtain the consistency you like. Set aside.

3. Preheat oven to 200°C (400°F). Rub pumpkin or butternut wedges with a dash of light olive oil. Roast for 30 minutes or until wedges are softened and caramelised.

4. Prepare syrup. Place sugar and water in a pot and bring to the boil. When sugar dissolves, add gingko nuts, vanilla essence and rum. Cook for a while longer to thicken the syrup.

5. To serve: place yam mash in a glass bowl. Add a couple of wedges of roasted pumpkin or butternut squash. Spoon gingko nuts and syrup over to glaze, and serve immediately.

serves 5-6

pear crisp with cranberries and orange peel

Call it a crisp or a crumble, but these fruit desserts baked with a crisp topping are perfect for healthy eating, with a few strategic substitutions. I made one with pears recently because I was attracted to the baby pears that were out in the market, though in the end the thrifty side of me prevailed. How could I pay the same price for a fruit that was half the usual size? So I picked the large ones.

Still large or small, a pear is a thing of beauty. Its shape calls to mind the most womanly of figures, appealing and winsome. More than eye appeal, a bowl of the fruit left out in the kitchen will scent the entire room as they ripen.

Nowadays with the varieties that flood the market, one cannot help but be enticed by the green, brown and red pears, aside from the baby ones, which appear to be Packhams. These are green pears, native to Australia, and if you look carefully they are less symmetrical in shape with a larger squat base. Its flesh, however, is sweet and its texture firm. It also keeps well. Unlike most fruit, pears improve in flavour and taste after being picked. Keep yours out in the open until they ripen. Store them after that in the refrigerator. I picked Packhams because they are easily available and hold their shape well after cooking.

While we know that most fruit is healthy, pears specifically provide fibre, vitamin C, natural sugar for energy and potassium for less than 100 calories for a medium-sized pear. As for the topping, I opted to make it wheat and dairy-free, so while you could opt for flour or breadcrumbs, I used oats. I also substituted the butter or margarine used in most recipes with olive oil, upping the health quotient tremendously. The rest of the ingredients were tossed in as well, simply because I like the crunch of nuts and the burst of flavour from the cranberries and the orange peel.

Alternatively you could add other ingredients such as spices, other nuts and various dried fruit to the basic crumble mix of oats, oil and sugar, giving more interest to this old classic.

Ripe Packham pears 4

Soft brown sugar 2 Tbsp

Lemon 1, grated for peel and squeezed for 1 tsp juice

Low-fat plain yoghurt

TOPPING

Whole oats 1 cup

Sliced almonds ¼ cup

Whole dried cranberries 2 Tbsp

Candied orange peel 2 Tbsp, chopped

Soft brown sugar ½ cup

Salt a pinch

Light olive oil ½ cup

1. Preheat oven to 180°C (350°F).

2. Peel and slice each pear lengthwise into 8 pieces. Toss with brown sugar and lemon juice until evenly coated. Add lemon peel. Leave in fridge to marinate.

3. Prepare topping. Combine oats, almonds, cranberries and chopped orange peel. Sprinkle sugar over, add a pinch of salt and pour over oil. Mix well.

4. Place pears in a baking dish. Cover with topping, spreading evenly.

5. Bake for 30 minutes. After 20 minutes, use a skewer to poke pears to test for tenderness. If topping is browning too fast, cover with a piece of aluminium foil and cook until pears are tender. Remember the pears will continue to cook in the residual heat after removing from the oven.

6. Serve immediately, with a dollop of yoghurt.

serves 6-8

poached peaches in white rum and lime syrup

There are many things to commend about this recipe. It is sinless— just fruit, improved by a splash of rum. It takes minutes to turn out and can be done in advance, so it is great for entertaining. Best of all, it is the kind of dessert for times when you want something cool and fresh in your mouth.

Poached fruit is not a new idea. Usually harder fruit such as pears and apples are poached, though increasingly cooks are poaching soft fruit such as figs, peaches and even mangoes. Incidentally poaching is a cooking method that is ideal for anyone on a low-fat diet, as it does not employ fat at all.

When poaching foods, however, do remember the food absorbs the flavour of the liquid so the seasoning is important. Taste it first before putting the food in to cook. Second, the heat must be kept at a simmer so that the flavour is not boiled out of the food. In this recipe, peaches are poached, then chilled. The white rum gives a whiff of the tropics while the garnish of red fruit such as cherries, strawberries or raspberries adds a visual counterpoint. Eating, after all, is also about pleasing the eye and not only the palate. That said, eating chilled poached peaches is to put a mouthful of sweet coolness in your mouth—the fruit slips down your throat in a refreshing finish!

Peaches come from China and are indeed associated with all good things such as fertility and affection. More than good associations however, a peach is a parcel of wellness. It is full of vitamins A (that combats the effects of aging), C and also of fibre, B vitamins and potassium. Thanks to the beta carotene found in it, a peach can also help build a strong immune system.

Unfortunately, we seldom can buy peaches at their best. They are picked before their prime and flown to our markets and depending on the timing, they may be ripe (or not) when you buy them. Even if ripe, the flesh of some fruit may be disappointingly cotton-y and dry. But with this recipe, you can turn less than perfect fruit into something quite memorable. You can use yellow or white peaches, but if white, add some strawberry jam to the poaching liquid to add a rosy tint. Even a beautiful peach needs make-up at times.

White or yellow peaches 4

Dried or fresh cherries, strawberries or raspberries a handful

Low-fat yoghurt (optional)

Fresh mint leaves for garnish

POACHING LIQUID

White sugar 1 cup

Water 2 cups

Vanilla pod 1, split, or use 1 tsp vanilla essence

White rum ½ cup

Lime ½, squeezed for juice

Strawberry jam (optional) 2 Tbsp

1. Prepare poaching liquid. Place sugar, water, vanilla pod or essence and rum in a pot large enough to accommodate peaches. Heat until sugar dissolves, then add lime juice and place peaches into the pot. If using white peaches, add strawberry jam to colour the poaching liquid.

2. Put a small plate over peaches to hold them down into the liquid. Cook over gentle heat for about 15 minutes and test the texture of the peaches by inserting the tip of a knife gently. They should be soft but not mushy.

3. Remove peaches with a slotted spoon and allow to cool.

4. The skin of the peaches should be quite easy to remove by now. Cut into half and remove the stone within.

5. Return peaches to poaching liquid and add fresh or dried cherries, strawberries or raspberries. Cool before leaving to steep for a few hours in the fridge.

6. To serve, divide peach halves in prepared serving bowl and spoon syrup over. Add cherries or berries, a dollop of yoghurt if liked, and garnish with mint leaves.

serves 8

yoghurt lemon pot

Only the English could have come up with this sweet idea. Take fresh strawberries, add whipped cream and break crisp meringues over it. You then dunk your spoon into this mess to stir it up before you eat a mouthful of a sweet, tart and rich confection. And let me assure you, it tastes better than it sounds. In fact I have never forgotten my first taste of Eton Mess, as it is called, although I really do not like too much cream in anything.

I decided to make the Eton Mess less harmful. So I substituted low-fat yoghurt for the cream, added lemon curd for lemony fragrance and tartness, some mandarin segments for freshness and finally, meringues for crunch. And it worked. I got a light, aromatic, fragrant yet satisfying dessert, despite the low-fat switches.

Instead, you can gloat over the healthful yoghurt that forms the bulk of this lemon pot and the fresh fruit that is added as well, adding not only colour and taste, but also fibre and vitamin C. Yoghurt, which dates back more than 4,000 years, is milk that has been fermented and curdled by "friendly" bacteria. Thanks also to these bacteria, especially acidophilus, yoghurt is believed to reduce the risk of intestinal infection by harmful organisms such as salmonella and E coli and improve digestion for those who are lactose-intolerant. For these reasons alone, my yoghurt-loving friends will eat a cup a day, and probably less for the fact that they are also downing 400 mg of calcium in every cup, 8 g of protein, as much potassium as a banana, as well as riboflavin (vitamin B2), phosphorus, and magnesium.

When cooking yoghurt, just make sure that you treat it gently, heating it only over low heat. I like to stir it in at the end of the recipe so that the healthy bacteria are not destroyed. The best yoghurt will have only live cultures and milk (full cream or skimmed) on the list of ingredients. The longer the list of ingredients, the more calories and fillers you get and the less of yoghurt nutrition.

In this dessert, the only two less than healthful additions are meringues and lemon curd. Add more or less of each depending on how strict you are about your diet. You must know, however, that meringues are made from only egg white and sugar. They can be made from scratch, of course, but can also be bought packed in boxes in gourmet supermarkets. Ditto for the lemon curd.

Low-fat plain yoghurt 100 g (3½ oz)

Good-quality lemon curd 1 Tbsp

Mandarin orange 1, peeled, seeded and separated into segments

Ready-made cup-sized meringues 1

1. Spoon out enough yoghurt to fill a third of a large glass serving bowl. Add a swirl of lemon curd, followed by another layer of yoghurt.

2. Add orange segments. Top with meringues, crumbled into the glass.

3. Serve immediately and instruct guests to mix everything together before plunging in with a spoon.

serves 1-2

kaffir lime granita and jelly

Nothing does it better than a mouthful of coolness that comes from a frozen ice or a soft slippery jelly on a hot day.

Both are childhood delights—I remember freezing some cola in the ice tray and making jelly from store-bought jelly crystals during the hot June holidays and waiting impatiently for the first to freeze and the other to set. And I am still doing it, though for different reasons. Both ice and jelly are wonderfully low-fat desserts. Put the two together in a glass and I get a delicious contrast of textures. Add a dollop of (low-fat, of course) yoghurt and creaminess is found in the mix. And if I flavour both ice and jelly mixtures with exotic flavours such as kaffir lime and lemon grass, I introduce a tropical element to the cool mouthful.

If you like frozen desserts, do leave a jug of syrup chilled in the fridge, then just add whatever fruit purée or juice you fancy and freeze, for your very own flavoured ice. While I was happy in the past with just a flavoured ice cube, nowadays I prefer the ice to emerge fluffy and soft, which describes an Italian granita to the tee.

Unlike the fine crystals of a sorbet, a granita is coarser-grained. Both sorbet and granita do not have milk or cream, making them great for a low-fat diet. They use just ice, fruit, sugar and sometimes herbs or even nut milks. And it is this coarse-grained texture that makes this Italian ice easier to turn out, even without an ice cream maker. I just use a fork to scratch at the formed icy surface. And it is the granitas of the Aeolian island of Salina off Sicily that draw people from everywhere.

Here at a rather down-home bar that does not match its reputation, ices of the most intense flavours are produced including the signature limone (made from the sweet and fragrant lemons of the island). The locals eat this ice with a brioche, a rich buttery bun, for breakfast! Back home, I substituted this with a chocolate biscuit. And of course since this is a tropical island, I used kaffir lime and lemon grass, so luxuriant in my garden, as flavourings instead.

Water 1 litre (32 fl oz / 4 cups)

Kaffir lime leaves 30, crushed

Lemon grass 2 stalks, ends trimmed, hard outer leaves removed and flattened

White sugar 2 cups

White rum 85 ml (2½ fl oz / ⅓ cup)

Large limes 3, grated for zest and squeezed for juice

Gelatine powder 5 g (⅙ oz)

Low-fat plain yoghurt (optional) 1 tub

Store-bought chocolate almond biscuits 1 packet

1. Bring water, together with kaffir lime leaves and lemon grass to the boil. Add sugar, stirring to dissolve. Leave mixture to simmer for about 15 minutes to develop the flavours. Add white rum.

2. Strain mixture, pressing down on the kaffir lime leaves and lemon grass stalks to release juices into a bowl. Add lime juice.

3. Pour half the mixture into a flat pan and place in the freezer to make the granita.

4. Add gelatine to the rest of the syrup, whisking until dissolved. Leave to cool a little.

5. Pour cooled jelly mixture into serving glasses, filling a third of the glasses. Allow to set in the fridge.

6. Scrape the granita with a fork to break up the ice-crystals as soon as it forms to get a smoother texture. Do this every 20 minutes or so until there is no more liquid and what remains is just soft flavoured ice.

7. To assemble: When jelly has set, top with a layer of granita and add a dollop of yoghurt, if liked. Scatter lime zest over and serve with a chocolate almond biscuit or the side.

serves 8

rosy with
health

a red menu for chinese new year:

the colour red is associated with celebrations and festivities, but behind that ancient tradition, lies some modern principles for good nutrition.

few know that colour in food also indicates lots of good things found in them. indeed the more colourful the food, the richer it is in antioxidants, which is why you should have as multi-coloured a diet as possible.

the bright orange colour of carrots and mangoes, for example, is a dead giveaway of the beta-carotenes found in them while the reds associated with watermelons, tomatoes and strawberries reveal the presence of that powerful antioxidant, lycopene. size does not matter, for the tiny red wolfberry is rich with vitamin c and beta-carotene, and the blue of the blueberry points to another antioxidant, anthocyanin, found in it.

antioxidants not only help to protect against diseases such as cancer and heart disease but also ensure good skin, hair, eyes and nails. did you know that the capsaicin in red chillies accounts not only for its fire, but may also fire you up, boosting metabolic rates, at least for the short time!

so richly coloured foods are desirable for many reasons and not only to brighten up a celebration.

a red menu for chinese new year

crab and chilli jelly

It's the new year, so let us serve red foods to match the season.

Think of pink crabs and prawns, red salmon and snapper, red cranberries, strawberries, wolfberries, and red vegetables such as beetroot, chillies, carrot and even red lettuce. With such an assortment on offer, I came up with a menu that is not only red in colour but is also rosy with health.

Think of it. The vibrant colours found on this festive table mean that antioxidants abound. The emphasis on seafood such as crab and salmon means that you need not worry about your mineral or protein levels while salmon delivers healthy omega-3 oils to the system.

Vitamin C is plentiful, thanks to the presence of chilli (which also has anti-inflammatory capsaicin in it) strawberries and red cabbage in this meal. And best of all, none of the fruit and vegetables is cooked—which means none of their nutrition has been destroyed by heat.

But since healthy eating is seldom a high priority during a festive season, let me assure you that taste is not wanting in these recipes. How could anyone resist a whole crab claw encased in a spicy red jelly? Or a whole side of salmon slathered with a delicious dressing of ginger and lemon? (Incidentally, this dressing cuts through the richness of this fish.) While I also add pickled cucumbers and coriander oil to dress the plate for the occasion, you could omit these if you are pushed for time.

Finally, strawberries in a salad is not so extreme a notion. Aside from its red colour, here it balances out the sweetness of the cabbage and provides a welcome tartness. Indeed this is a meal that is not just a feast for the eyes but also for the whole body.

Raw crab claws 10, or peeled cooked crabmeat, available from supermarkets

Large red chillies 3–4, or use bird's eye chillies if you want a spicier flavour

Cranberry-flavoured jelly crystals 1 packet, about 170 g (6 oz)

Salt a pinch

Light mayonnaise

Crushed black pepper to taste

Fresh parsley for garnish

1. Place crab claws on a plate and steam, covered, for 15 minutes in a wok. Cool. You can use the claws whole, or peeled in chunks.

2. Cut chillies diagonally into 10 or more pieces and remove just the loose seeds using the tip of a knife. This is to prevent the jelly from being dotted with too many seeds.

3. Dissolve jelly crystals in 2 cups boiling water, stirring until crystals dissolve. Add a pinch of salt and another 2 cups of cold water. Divide solution into 8 small glass bowls or jelly cups.

4. Place one crab claw or a tablespoon of crabmeat, if using, and chilli pieces into jelly mixture and refrigerate to set, for about 3 hours.

5. To serve, place a dollop of mayonnaise on top, sprinkle with black peppeer to taste and garnish with a parsley floret.

serves 8-10

seared salmon with ginger and lemon dressing

Salmon fillet 1.4 kg (3 lb 3 oz)

Cucumber 1

PICKLING BRINE

Water 1 cup

Rice vinegar ½ cup

Salt ¼ tsp

Sugar 1 tsp

LEMON AND GINGER DRESSING

Ginger 3 large knobs, peeled and cut into pieces

Lemon 1, peel left intact, seeded and cut into pieces

Salt 2 tsp

Olive oil ½ cup

CORIANDER OIL

Coriander (cilantro) leaves 1 bunch

Olive oil ½ cup

Salt ½ tsp

GARNISH

Dried wolfberries a handful, reconstituted in hot water to soften

1. Buy salmon fillet on day of cooking. Choose the freshest one available and ask the fishmonger to fillet it for you, removing the skin and the bones. Feel the surface of the fish and if there are any remaining bones, use a pair of tweezers to remove. Leave fish covered in the refrigerator until needed. Slice the cucumber thinly and leave, uncovered, in the fridge for a few hours to dry.

2. Meanwhile, prepare pickling brine. Combine all ingredients in a pot and bring to the boil. Remove from heat and leave aside to cool. Place cucumber slices into the brine and leave until needed. You can do this ahead of time.

3. Prepare ginger and lemon dressing. Blend all ingredients in a food processor, then heat mixture in a pot until ginger and lemon pieces soften and caramelise. Leave aside until use.

4. Prepare coriander oil. Blend all ingredients in a food processor. And leave aside until use.

5. Using an oil spray, spray the surface of a grill pan with oil and heat pan under an oven grill until smoking hot. Place salmon on the pan to sear, then place pan on the topmost rung of the hot grill for 3–5 minutes, if you like rare doneness, or else cook it for 15 minutes.

6. To serve, top salmon with ginger-lemon dressing and garnish with wolfberries. Lay pickled cucumber slices around or on the side and drizzle coriander oil over.

serves 4-5

red cabbage and strawberry salad

BLACK VINEGAR SYRUP

Chinese black vinegar ½ cup

Brown sugar ½ cup

DRESSING

Canola oil ½ cup

Sesame oil 1 tsp

Sugar 1 tsp

Rice vinegar 2 Tbsp

Light soy sauce 1 tsp

Salt ¼ tsp

SALAD

Strawberries 1 punnet, about 250 g (9 oz), hulled

Red cabbage ½ head, shredded finely

Red lettuce 1 head, leaves separated and washed

Toasted sesame seeds (optional) for garnish

Roasted almond slivers (optional) for garnish

1. Prepare black vinegar syrup. Combine black vinegar and sugar in a small pot. Bring to the boil, then reduce heat and leave to simmer until thickened. Leave aside.

2. Prepare dressing. Combine ingredients in a bowl and whisk with a fork to emulsify the mixture. Leave aside.

3. Wipe strawberries with a cloth. Do not wash or the flavour will leach away. Slice lengthwise and leave aside.

4. Place shredded cabbage in a bowl and pour over dressing. Toss to ensure that leaves are well coated.

5. Assemble salad. Place lettuce leaves on a plate. Lay strawberries on top, overlapping in concentric rings. Place a mound of dressed cabbage leaves in the middle. Garnish with toasted sesame seeds and roasted almonds slivers, if liked.

6. Using a spoon, drizzle black vinegar syrup over the lot and serve at once.

serves 8-10

salmon dumplings

This is a time of largesse and what better way to celebrate Chinese New Year than by going supersize!

Instead of that tired classic of salmon *yu sheng*, I am going to serve the same fish, but in a different form. It should be terribly grand for guests to be presented with these over-sized dumplings sitting in a most flavoursome stock, as a first course.

Despite the size, the filling for the dumplings is very healthful with lots of omega-3 fats, thanks to the salmon found in it. For those who do not know, omega-3 fats found in fish is supposed to reduce inflammation in our bodies. And this is important because inflammation is turning out to be the source of many health problems, including heart disease, diabetes, some types of cancers and arthritis.

Fairly recent research even points to the potential of omega-3 fats to help slow cognitive problems such as Alzheimer's disease. But of course that is not the reason why we are eating salmon this season. It helps that it is a red fish though. And the festive colour shows through very prettily even when encased in a wrapper. The best reason is that it tastes luxuriously rich despite being healthy, which a great reason for eating anything!

Don't bother to make your dumpling wraps from scratch. The supermarket cold section sells very good round dumpling wrappers in packets. Instead of using just one wrap per dumpling, use two—one as a base and the other to cover the filling. Since the fish is wrapped, it would be hard to overcook it, but still, do remove the dumpling the moment it floats up when boiling. And do coat the cooked dumplings with some oil to prevent sticking later. I use an oil spray to do this without fuss.

Finally, garnish the dumplings with lots of shredded ginger and spring onion and if liked, also with a dip of Chinese red vinegar. That should whet the appetite or maybe that is not a good thing during this season of largesse!

STOCK

Homemade or canned chicken stock 1 litre (32 fl oz / 4 cups)

Dried mini-sized scallops 10, rinsed under a tap

Dried wolfberries 1 Tbsp, reconstituted in water to soften

Rice wine 2 Tbsp

FILLING

Boneless salmon steak 200 g (7 oz)

Salt a pinch

Ground white pepper to taste

Rice wine 1 Tbsp

Round wheat dumpling wrappers (the largest you can find) 24

Dried shredded Chinese mushrooms 1 cup, reconstituted in water to soften

Ginger 1 thumb-sized knob, peeled and shredded (set some aside for garnish)

DIPPING SAUCE AND GARNISH

Spring onion (scallion) 1–2, shredded for garnish

Chinese red vinegar enough as a dipping sauce

1. Boil chicken stock with scallops and wolfberries. After 30 minutes of simmering, add rice wine. Remove from heat and keep warm. If using homemade stock, add 1 tsp salt to taste.

2. Remove skin from salmon and slice. Season with salt, pepper and rice wine. Set fish aside to marinate.

3. Dust a board, or clean work surface with flour. Place dumpling wrapper on it. Place a spoonful of salmon slices in centre of wrapper. Top with mushrooms and ginger. Wet edges of wrapper with water and cover with another dumpling wrapper. Press the two edges together to seal. Place dumplings on a floured plate and repeat until all ingredients are used up.

4. Heat a pot of water and when boiling, reduce heat and add dumplings carefully, 2–3 at a time. Dumplings are cooked when they float to the surface.

5. Divide dumplings among prepared soup plates and ladle over stock. Garnish with spring onions and ginger and serve a small saucer of red Chinese vinegar as a dip, if desired.

serves 4-5

glossary

basmati rice

Basmati rice grains are long and increase considerably in length when cooked. They require slightly more water than Thai or Japanese rice varieties to cook. When cooked, the texture should be dry, fluffy, and aromatic. Basmati rice figures prominently in Indian cuisine, and brown and white varieties are sold. Though less common, brown basmati has a stronger flavour and contains more fibre.

binjai fruit

The *binjai* fruit is a species of mango that grows in Singapore, Malaysia, Brunei, Papua New Guinea and The Philippines. Also known as Malaysian mango, *binjai* fruit has thin brown skin and creamy, yellow-white flesh. It is soft to the touch when ripe, and has a sweet, sour and tangy flavour.

bottled artichokes

Fresh artichokes are not easily available in Singapore, so bottled artichokes make a good substitute. Bottled artichokes are usually marinated in olive oil and a mixture of herbs and spices. The marinating liquid can also double up as a flavourful dressing. Some marinating liquids may have a higher salt content; if you find them too salty, rinse the artichoke hearts before use.

brown rice

Brown rice has a mild, nutty flavour, and is becoming increasingly popular due to the fact that it is more healthful than white rice. The coloured outer layer of brown rice contains bran and germ, which in turn contain extra fibre, making it chewy and more nutritious. Brown rice usually requires a longer cooking time, and will not have the same tender and fluffy texture as cooked white rice does.

butternut squash

Also known as butternut pumpkin, butternut is a variety of winter squash. Its light, tan-coloured skin yields yellow-orange flesh that is sweet and creamy. Butternut squash is suitable for roasting and making soups. It is rich in vitamins and carotene, and is low in fat content. When choosing a squash, ensure that the skin is smooth and even, with no blemishes or mouldy spots.

century eggs

Century eggs are chicken or duck eggs that have been preserved in over a period of time ranging from several weeks to months (see article page 33). They are characterised by their strong, pungent odour and flavour. In Chinese cuisine, they are chilled and served as a starter, or used as an ingredient in porridge, bean curd and vegetable dishes.

fish floss

Meat floss is made by stewing tough cuts of meat, marinated in soy sauce for lengthy periods of time to break down the elasticin and collagen in it. After that happens, the meat is oven-dried, then dry-fried until it becomes fluffy and coarse. Fish floss is prepared the same way but takes a considerably shorter time to prepare, due to the low elasticin and collagen content. A good alternative for non-meat eaters, fish floss is a flavourful topping for congee, and is also a popular filling in Chinese-style pastries.

hon shimeji mushrooms

Hon shimeji mushrooms are a variety of shimeji, an increasingly popular Japanese mushroom. They come in various shades of colour, ranging from white, light tan colours to brown. They have a clean, slightly buttery flavour, and a meaty texture.

kokum

Kokum is native to the Western and coastal parts of India, and Sri Lanka. The bright reddish-pruple fruits become darker as they ripen. The rind is dried and sold as a flavouring agent for soups, curries and other dishes, lending a distinct sweet-sour flavour. it is also used to make a cooling, refreshing drink. The dried rinds should be stored in an airtight container in a cool, dry place.

lemon grass

Lemon grass is a highly aromatic herb with long, slender leaves and bulbous stems. The stems contain glands that release pungent oils when sliced or bruised, which impart a distinct, lemony flavour to the dish it is added to.

ricotta salata

Ricotta salata is basically a form of salted sheep's milk cheese that is pressed, dried and salted. it has a creamy, slightly spongy texture and a salty, milky flavour. Sold in blocks, *ricotta salata* can be grated over salads and pastas for added flavour.

vietnamese rice paper rolls

Vietnamese rice paper rolls are made from water and rice flour. It is translucent and thin, and should be briefly soaked in water to soften slightly before use.

abalone mushrooms

More commonly known as oyster mushrooms, abalone mushrooms have a distinct, fan-like shape, meaty stems and smooth texture. Their flavour resembles that of oysters. Canned abalone mushrooms are commonly available in supermarkets, should fresh ones be unavailable.

wild rice

also known as Indian rice, wild rice are grass seeds from an aquatic plant related to the rice family. Although it is not categorically a rice, it is used in much the same way. Wild rice is also more flavourful than rice, chewier in terms of texture and contains more protein and nutrients.

wolfberries

Wolfberries are small, red berries of the boxthorn plant. They have a pleasant, herbal sweetness, and are a popular ingredient in Chinese soups, stews and dessert soups. They are native to East Asia and Inner Mongolia, and are rich in carotene and vitamin C. Wolfberries are sold in dried form.

yunnan ham

Yunnan ham is a dried, cured ham from the province of Yunnan in China. It adds a rich flavour and depth to soups and dishes, and is sold in different grades according to quality.

furikake

Furikake is a Japanese condiment that is used as a topping for rice. The variety of ingredients in a *furikake* mix can vary widely. A basic mixture consists of dried, ground fish, seasoning, salt, sugar and seaweed. Most *furikake* mixes may scontain monosodium glutamate for added flavour; if you are concerned about that, do check the nutritional label on *furikake* packets in the supermarkets before purchase.

index

weights and measures

quantities for this book are given using the metric system. standard measurements used are: 1 tsp = 5 ml, 1 tbsp = 15 ml, 1 cup = 250 ml. all measures are level unless otherwise stated.

liquid and volume measures

metric	imperial	american
5 ml	1/6 fl oz	1 tsp
10 ml	1/3 fl oz	1 dsp
15 ml	1/2 fl oz	1 tbsp
60 ml	2 fl oz	1/4 cup (4 tbsp)
85 ml	2 1/2 fl oz	1/3 cup
90 ml	3 fl oz	3/8 cup (6 tbsp)
125 ml	4 fl oz	1/2 cup
180 ml	6 fl oz	3/4 cup
250 ml	8 fl oz	1 cup
300 ml	10 fl oz (1/2 pint)	1 1/4 cups
375 ml	12 fl oz	1 1/2 cups
435 ml	14 fl oz	1 3/4 cups
500 ml	16 fl oz	2 cups
625 ml	20 fl oz (1 pint)	2 1/2 cups
750 ml	24 fl oz (1 1/5 pints)	3 cups
1 litre	32 fl oz (1 3/5 pints)	4 cups
1.25 litres	40 fl oz (2 pints)	5 cups
1.5 litres	48 fl oz (2 2/5 pints)	6 cups
2.5 litres	80 fl oz (4 pints)	10 cups

dry measures

metric	imperial
30 g	1 ounce
45 g	1 1/2 ounces
55 g	2 ounces
70 g	2 1/2 ounces
85 g	3 ounces
100 g	3 1/2 ounces
110 g	4 ounces
125 g	4 1/2 ounces
140 g	5 ounces
280 g	10 ounces
450 g	16 ounces (1 pound)
500 g	1 pound, 1 1/2 ounces
700 g	1 1/2 pounds
800 g	1 3/4 pounds
1 kg	2 pounds, 3 ounces
1.5 kg	3 pounds, 4 1/2 ounces
2 kg	4 pounds, 6 ounces

oven temperature

	°c	°f	gas regulo
very slow	120	250	1
slow	150	300	2
moderately slow	160	325	3
moderate	180	350	4
moderately hot	190/200	370/400	5/6
hot	210/220	410/440	6/7
very hot	230	450	8
super hot	250/290	475/550	9/10

length

metric	imperial
0.5 cm	1/4 inch
1 cm	1/2 inch
1.5 cm	3/4 inch
2.5 cm	1 inch

abbreviation

tsp	teaspoon
tbsp	tablespoon
	gram
	kilogramme
ml	millilitre